# THE IRRESISTIBLE ATTRACTION OF
# DIVINITY

SWAMI AMRITASWARUPANANDA PURI

Mata Amritanandamayi Center
San Ramon, California, United States

# The Irresistible Attraction of Divinity
By Swami Amritaswarupananda Puri

Published by:
   Mata Amritanandamayi Center
   P.O. Box 613
   San Ramon, CA 94583-0613, USA

In India:
   www.amritapuri.org
   inform@amritapuri.org

In USA:
   www.amma.org

In Europe:
   www.amma-europe.org

# CONTENTS

| Introduction | 7 |

1 | Amma's Sankalpa | 16 |

2 | Epitome of Vedanta | 31 |

3 | Call And Response | 49 |

4 | The Divine Music That Woke Me Up | 72 |

5 | Sahasrapade Namah | 87 |

6 | Guru Is God Embodied | 99 |

7 | A Heart As Expansive As The Sky | 131 |

8 | Birthday Gift | 148 |

9 | A Catalyst Beyond Compare | 168 |

10 | The Compelling Power Of Selflessness | 181 |

11 | Ever Established In Sahaja Samadhi | 197 |

12 | The All-Encompassing Nature
Of The Guru | 207 |

13 | Torrential Grace | 229 |

14 | Come Quickly, Darling Children | 247 |

# DEDICATION

*dhyāyāmaḥ suvibhātabhānuvadanām*
*sāndrāvabōdhātmikām*
*tattvajñānavibhūṣitāmabhayadām*
*tacchabdavidyōtikām*
*mandasmērasubhāṣitairnatikṛtām*
*sarvārtividdvamsikām*
*brahmānandaparāyaṇāmatulitā-*
*mambāmṛtākhyām parām*

We meditate on Amma, whose countenance is as radiant as the rising sun, who is pure consciousness embodied, who is adorned with the jewel of spiritual wisdom, who grants refuge to devotees, who kindles the knowledge of the Supreme in the hearts of disciples, who, with her sweet smile and ambrosial words, dispels the sorrows of the distressed, who is ever established in Brahman, the Supreme, who is peerless, and who has become renowned by the name Amrita.

*ōm prēmāmṛtānandamayyai
nityam namō namaḥ*

# | INTRODUCTION

Love is the only thing in the whole world that has an irresistible attraction. It is the most predominant feeling inherent in all living beings. Regardless of our background, nationality, language and the section of society we belong to, the power of love remains common to all of humanity, perhaps to the entire creation.

Though the energy behind love is the same, it manifests diversely depending on each person's *samskara* (latent tendencies). This is how Amma puts it, "For a scientist, love means protons and neutrons. A poet or orator considers words as love, while food is love for some. Love for the near and dear ones is common. Color is love for an artist. A baby's love is for its mother, and for a honeybee it is flowers. But for a devotee, God is love. Similarly, for a disciple, the guru is love."

Human beings are considered to be the most evolved of all species. So, besides expressing this beautiful energy of love at the physical and emotional levels, we should also direct it towards a greater purpose and gravitate towards a higher goal. What is this goal? It is to realize the reality about our existence, the very fabric we are made of. Allow me to quote Amma's words. She says, "Love is the only language that everyone, including plants, animals and even insentient objects can understand. It is a universal language. Love is the biggest purifier and greatest transformer."

Amma's ashram in Amritapuri has two dogs: Tumban and Bhakti, male and female, respectively. They were rehabilitated from the streets as puppies. If anyone at all enjoys absolute physical freedom in the ashram, it is these two dogs. They have access everywhere, including Amma's room, her bed and the darshan stage. No one questions their authority. They have a very special connection with Amma. The way they conduct themselves in front of Amma and her love and care for them have an inconceivable aspect to it. It is so obvious. Watching them, one cannot help wondering, 'Who are these dogs?'

Tumban and Bhakti meticulously attend the morning archana (chanting of the *Sri Lalita Sahasranama*, 1000 names of Goddess Lalita Parameswari, followed by singing of the *Mahishasura Mardini Stotram*) and the evening bhajans along with all the ashram residents. When Amma sings, she makes sure that there is sufficient space by the side of her *peetham* (seat) for Tumban to lie down comfortably. While Tumban shares the same seat with Amma, Bhakti crawls under her seat. Bhakti never sits on the peetham, even if there is space, even if Tumban is absent...!

Another aspect of their bond with Amma is the immense longing both dogs have to get Amma's love and affection, especially Tumban. He often expresses his desire to be loved. On many occasions, he approaches Amma wanting to be caressed. Here is a short description of what he does. He raises his foreleg and gently lifts or touches Amma's hand, gesturing her to rub his head. Of course, Amma always obliges Tumban's request. When she stops, he again does the same gesture. The point is, even animals and plants respond to true love.

Love is an alchemist. It has the power to change anything and everything. It gives individuality even to inert objects. Amma says, "We name our dogs and cats, don't we? The name creates a big change. A shift takes place in our inner world. The animal or bird suddenly becomes an individual.

They gain a personality." The love within us is the power that bestows an identity to the pet by raising its status to one who is cherished. The dog, cat, or bird undergoes a transformation in our mind, even though it was just one among hundreds of pets in some random pet shop or shelter until a few minutes ago! This, indeed, is the real miracle.

Every tree at Amma's ashram in San Ramon, California, has a name. The name gives a special status to the tree. This also brings about a change in perception for the people living there, as well as the visiting devotees. Little children name their toys, their barbie dolls, their teddy bears, etc. Once they name the doll, it is not an inert object any more. For them, the doll becomes alive. It has feelings, hunger, thirst, need to sleep and so forth. The children treat the doll like a human being.

This spontaneous urge to feel love, to express love and to be love is innate in children, adults, animals, and plants (albeit not as visibly).

Love is as important as the air we breathe. It is essential to the well-being of our existence. Nay. It is the foundation of our true being, our essence, the very substratum of our existence. Love is the purest form of energy. The source of this everlasting energy is within us. As we go deeper and deeper into the wellspring of love, the secret chambers of our heart open up. The more love in our heart, the more wonders will take place in our life. We call these 'miracles,' 'amazing experiences,' or 'impossible feats.'

Regardless of the name we use, the fact is, love has taken us closer to our own Self, closer to God, closer to creation. When we fall in love with creation, it responds by falling in love with us. Gradually, this attraction unfolds into an extraordinary love affair, a bonding embrace, which eventually blends the two into one. That love affair is the beginning of an inexhaustible mutual sharing.

When the love within us awakens and blossoms fully, we automatically become in tune with the universe. Many eminent scientists today and in the past are great admirers of the universe. They view the universe with utter wonderment. The depth of their love inspires them to dive deep into the mysteries therein. The distinguished scientist Carl Sagan remarked, "For small creatures such as we, the vastness is bearable only through love."

In Amma, we see an entirely different dimension of this love. She has raised it to the state of transcendence, beyond all limits. Thus, Amma is a *'Brahmavid,'* a knower of the absolute consciousness, where knowing and being are one and the same. Permanently established in the state of *sahaja samadhi* (the highest spiritual realization), Amma has come to help others who are in search of the Truth. In her we see the immeasurable profundity and the mystifying expansiveness of supreme love.

Even though we see Amma constantly engaged in various activities such as running the eight-campus Amrita University, advising on the scientific research the students and faculty conduct, adopting the poorest rural villages throughout India and helping the villagers advance in the direction of sustainable development, or giving darshan to thousands upon thousands of people every day, she is always one with the transcendental reality. She engages in each activity peacefully and blissfully.

When a knower of Brahman choses to be in the world out of infinite compassion for humanity, they will be an irresistible divine attraction.

Nothing—neither human nor supernatural forces—can stop that enchanting power of a Satguru, an enlightened or Self-realized spiritual master, who, out of sheer compassion helps people to cross over the ocean of grief. It is like the earth's gravitational force. Everything moves towards them.

The Satguru is like a magnifying glass. Our smallest negativities will be amplified in their presence. There is no hiding the truth from the guru. That presence, indeed, is the most conducive atmosphere for a *sadhak*, a spiritual seeker, endowed with an intense desire to realize the God within, to explore the unknown world of spirituality. Like an adroit and knowledgeable travel guide, Amma will guide us on the journey. Throughout this voyage, our one and only companion will be the Satguru. The shower of her uninterrupted and pure motherly love, the infinite wisdom that she offers, the depth of her understanding, and the divine beauty of her realization makes the journey a celebration. At the same time, Amma also disciplines us with the affection of a great and remarkable parent, enabling us to grow beyond our lower tendencies, the *vasanas* that impede our path.

The first step of this journey is the awakening of the inherent love within us. Having rekindled the light of love within, Amma also makes sure that this flame of love remains ablaze. In the crystalline luminosity of that love, we go through a purifying process. Gradually, as the love within us is purified, our awareness, our consciousness level, also increases. It awakens the inner potential and opens up unknown realms of existence.

The guru-disciple bonding is the rarest of all relationships. It can only be told through stories, personal experiences, scriptural quotes and so forth. That is what this book is all about. It is a compilation, an adaptation, of some of my public talks and articles.

The main points discussed in the essays include: the Satguru and the universality of the guru principle, the all-encompassing nature of the guru, why the Satguru and God are one and the same, the uniqueness of the guru-disciple relationship, the importance of innocent love, grace, the irresistible attraction of the guru, and other spiritual topics.

I will consider myself blessed if this book ignites sparks in the readers' minds. Most importantly, every word of this book, every single incident, is a small reflection of the Satguru Amma within me. What I am now, if at all I have achieved anything, is only because of Amma's infinite grace and guidance. Without her, I am nothing.

This introduction would be incomplete if I didn't gratefully mention Sneha's (Karen Moawad) name. Her wholehearted and selfless assistance helped me edit this book. It is her love and devotion for Amma that inspired her to spend so much time and energy. I have no words to express my gratitude to her.

Let me conclude by quoting the late President of India, APJ Abdul Kalam, who was a prominent scientist and a great human being. He said, "When God pushes you to the edge of difficulty, trust him fully. Because, two things can happen. Either, He will catch you when you fall, or He will teach you how to fly." Amma not only teaches us how to soar high in the sky of God consciousness but also teaches us how to become one with it.

Swami Amritaswarupananda Puri

Mata Amritanandamayi Math

Amritapuri. Kollam, Kerala

India

# 1 | AMMA'S SANKALPA

People pour out their heart to Amma during darshan. While listening to their woes, Amma lovingly intones into their ears, *"Makkale, Amma sankalpikkam"* ("Children, Amma will make a *sankalpa* (divine resolve))." This counsel is quite familiar to devotees, not only in India, but all over the world. Many people ask, "Amma said that she would make a resolve. What does that mean? Does it mean she will 'think,' or that she will 'pray'?"

It is interesting to note before answering this question, that Hindus normally pray to the highest absolute God, Brahman, or to God's three manifestations: Brahma, the creator god; Vishnu, the preserver god; and Shiva, the god of dissolution (so that the creation cycle can start again). Or, they may pray to Vishnu's incarnations, Rama and Krishna, or to other deities such as Amma. When enlightened beings use the word, 'sankalpa,' it is not a mere 'thought.' Nor is it a 'prayer' the way we normally think of prayer. A 'sankalpa' is a very subtle and therefore very powerful intention that a Self-realized master alone can make, by exercising

his or her *Iccha Sakti*: the power of will to control, resolve or eliminate a certain harmful situation, or to create a positive change. Only an enlightened soul, who is beyond all likes and dislikes, who is one with the totality, is capable of doing this. The *Brihadaranyaka Upanishad* says:

*sō'kāmayata dvitīyō ma ātmā jāyētēti*

He willed, or God willed, may I have a second Self. (1.2.4)

This is how the creation, the world we see, came into being. The world is like the clothing of the Supreme Being. Hence, it is called, "second Self." When the Upanishad says "second Self," it is because of the innumerable names and forms that we see in the world. Therefore, there is a certain 'otherness' to this world. This reference of the "second Self" also indicates that the world is not the reality itself, but a reflection.

The realization of this oneness, the ultimate secret behind the diverse world of names and forms, enables the knower to exercise control over all five elements. Though they have control over the fundamental building material of the universe, such beings don't use their powers to disturb the established laws of the universe. In other words, the will of an enlightened soul and the will of the universe are the same, in perfect tune. A Self-realized master is also a *trikala jnani*, a knower of all three periods of time (past, present, and future). He or she can easily infuse pure energy into anything sentient or insentient, thereby uplifting them or fulfilling their spiritual and material wishes and goals, but definitely not harmful and selfish ones. So, a sankalpa is something that springs forth from the innermost being of a perfect master, a Satguru. The recipient of a sankalpa must also be qualified to receive and maintain the purity of the divine sankalpa.

This transmission of energy is called sankalpa. This energy is much stronger than matter, so much so that even impossible things become possible. Perhaps, we can refer to it as a 'command from the ultimate controller of elements.' Nonetheless, this should not be interpreted as the only purpose of Self-realized masters. One should also keep in mind that making a sankalpa involves numerous factors, mostly unseen, beyond our comprehension.

Basically, it is difficult to define the sankalpa of a great master such as Amma. It is a revelation, a blessed moment, or a situation that happens, maybe through an uplifting and blissful experience. The guru bestows it, knowing the heart of the devotee and the subtleties of his/her *dharma* and *karma* (i.e. nature from both a material and spiritual perspective).

Perhaps, one can say, it is a process by which the guru gives a fraction of God, a part of the guru's infinite energy, to the devotee or disciple, so that he or she can nurture it, like in a womb, meditate upon it, and gradually find fulfilment.

When Amma says that she will make a resolve, it also means that she will act in full knowledge of the rhythm, the cosmic order. In essence, the sankalpa of a *mahatma*, a perfect master, a Satguru beyond human comprehension, manifests as an inspiring and powerful experience.

Allow me to share an incident.

Thirty three years ago, in September of 1986, we were celebrating Amma's 33rd birthday at the old temple, known as the *kalari*, with a small gathering of renunciates and devotees. Amma had not yet traveled outside of India, but had recently accepted an invitation by some of the devotees to visit the United States. Amma had entrusted the task of arranging the overseas programs to Kusumam (Gretchen McGregor).

On the eve of her departure to the U.S., Kusumam bowed down to Amma seeking her blessing. Amma lovingly embraced her and said, "My daughter, ask for nothing. Everything will come to you."

"Amma's words to me on the eve of my departure would echo in my ear as I traversed the United States in preparation for Amma's first World Tour," recalls Kusumam.

Six months later, on 23rd March 1987, Swami Paramatmananda (Neil Rosner) and I were getting ready to leave for the U.S. to join Kusumam and pave the way for Amma's first World Tour. I was going to be away from Amma's physical presence for a full two months. Though my duty called me, I was feeling sad, a deep pain of separation. While taking leave, when I prostrated at Amma's feet, she held me close and compassionately whispered in my ears, "Son, Amma is with you; Amma's sankalpa is with you."

We set off on our journey. Our first stop was in Singapore. After two days of programs there, we flew to San Francisco and landed there on March 26th. From the airport, we drove straight to the home of Swami Paramatmananda's elder brother, Earl Rosner, in Oakland.

I still remember his house and its surroundings. The reason is that from the time I took leave of Amma and boarded the plane in Kochi, my heart was being churned by anguish. By the time I reached Oakland, the anguish had become a deep sorrow. Even though only a few days had passed, Earl's home was where I felt the pain of separation from Amma intensely.

Although winter was slowly bidding its farewell, it was still quite cold. From before dawn, when the first rays of the rising sun caressed the earth, until dusk, one could hear a medley of tunes from a variety of birds. The trees, which had shed their leaves during winter's onslaught, had begun to sprout tender leaves again. Flowering plants were slowly beginning to blossom. There were dazzling dewdrops on both leaves and flowers.

"I'm on the other side of the world. I'm separated from Amma by the distance between day and night," my heart ached. But *svadharma*, the work that Amma had entrusted me with, became a wake-up call: "I must prepare for Amma's visit."

We had scheduled a 40-day-long tour across the U.S. before Amma's sacred feet were to touch American soil. Programs had been planned in many places. Staying in Oakland for five days, we conducted programs in the San Francisco Bay Area. The rest of the tour was to start in the early morning of April 1st, first from Oakland to Seattle, and then back to Oakland. From there, we were going to Madison, Wisconsin, covering about 5,000 miles (12,000 kilometers) in all.

There were seven of us on this tour. We decided to load our luggage into the vehicle the night before the tour was scheduled to start. Jack Dawson, a devotee, had kindly donated the vehicle for our journey. But it had not arrived yet. Kusumam, who was waiting by the roadside, finally called out, "The vehicle has come. Let's start loading." That was when I saw the vehicle that was to carry us all on the long journey. I was dumbstruck. To be honest, I had expected a vehicle that was reasonably large and in fairly good condition. After all, this was the USA...! But what I saw parked in front of the house was a Dodge van, which looked like the old model standard van in India. In other words, it was an antiquated relic.

I had a doubt: was this really the vehicle? I looked at Kusumam. She cleared my doubt, "Yup, this is the one! We couldn't get anything else." Seeing that it looked as if it was ready for the junkyard, I almost blurted out, "Oh God! Will this van be able to take us on our tour?"

I immediately checked myself. No! Had not Amma given us her guarantee? "Son, Amma is with you, Amma has made a sankalpa." Why then these doubts and questions? This was Amma's will.

From behind, I heard Swami Paramatmananda saying, "Yeah, it's a real junker. But don't worry about how old it is or what it looks like. It's Amma's power that's going to run it! So, come on, let's start loading things."

It was my first foreign tour—in an unfamiliar world with a totally different culture and customs. There were only a handful of people to help. Yet, wasn't Amma with us? Wasn't her resolve going to help us? We surrendered to that faith and set out on our journey.

For the next 40 days, the van literally became our place of refuge, our home. Cooking, eating, sleeping, meditating, chanting, doing yoga exercises... everything was done inside it. It served us like a faithful friend.

"This vehicle will shudder to a halt anytime now. We might get stranded in a deserted place without any help. We will miss our programs!" Such fears often assailed us. If something like that had happened, we had nothing like a Plan B. Our faith in Amma alone was our Plan A, B and C. She was our sole companion. We encountered many obstructions and difficulties. Whenever we anxiously wondered, "What next?" some stranger would show up to help. Thus, Amma appeared in many names, forms and circumstances.

We continued the journey, crossing mountains and deserts, and passing through large cities and small towns. We narrated stories about Amma, shared experiences, sang bhajans and conducted satsang and meditation programs. We met and got to know many people who would help Amma's mission in the U.S. We spoke to them about the phenomenon that is Amma.

As if an obedient servant of an unseen power, our mount, "the great grandpa Dodge," continued carrying us for 40 days without sulking or whining. Gradually, our lives inside the van became suffused with an ashram atmosphere saturated by Amma's presence.

The trip was nearing its end. We reached our destination, Madison. From there, we were going to take a bus to Chicago. Thereafter, we were also scheduled to visit New York and Boston. Amma was going to reach San Francisco on May 18th. We had to get back there before that.

The day we arrived in Madison, our 'trusted servant' the Dodge van, as if having sincerely fulfilled the task that 'someone' had assigned, conked out. No matter how hard we tried, we could not get it to start again. Swami Paramatmananda, with palms joined together, said, "This can only be the divine sankalpa of Amma." It was indeed a revelation. To our surprise, we also found out that Jack Dawson, the person who offered the van for our travel was originally from Madison…! Somehow the Dodge van knew it was "home."

This experience was one of the many incidents that unfolded the meaning of 'divine sankalpa' for me. It dawned on us that the old vehicle wasn't just a conglomeration of insentient metal and engine. We couldn't see it like that anymore. For us, it seemed to be a living being, which obeyed the orders of an unknown and mysterious power. The change in our perception made a huge difference in our attitude towards the vehicle. Before leaving Madison, we performed arati, offered flowers, prostrated and bid farewell to that good friend, which was the visible manifestation of Amma's resolve, and which had worn itself out in fulfilling its assigned duty.

The buff-colored Dodge van was a great lesson and the perfect metaphor of surrender for each of us in our own way. We had no means to create a pre-tour, including a vehicle to travel. So when Jack Dawson offered his van, we knew that Amma was providing our 'unasked for' transport, though we initially branded it as a 'junker.' Yes, it was old and had over 100,00 miles, but as it carried out its 'assigned duty most dedicatedly and selflessly,' we began to see it as a majestic coach that materialized from nowhere, a perfect example to prove how a divine sankalpa can work wonders.

While traveling the thousands of miles required to complete the first 40 days of the pre-tour — from Oakland to Mt. Shasta, Miranda, Seattle, Santa Fe, Taos, Boulder, Chicago and Madison — we (Swami Paramatmananda, Kusumam and I) had no idea of the magnitude of the mission Amma wanted us to fulfil, and what would unfold in the future. We only knew we were to get the word out about Amma's imminent arrival. We were joyful, enthusiastic, inspired and meticulous in our sadhana as well.

Divine incarnations act according to definite goals. Their mind is as vast as the universe and as clear as the sky. They have no doubts or confusions. In order to realize their objectives, they can infuse a feeling or sensation (as distinguished from perception or thought) even into inert objects. If that resolve and blessing are with us, there is nothing we cannot do in all the worlds. That great power, which emerged from inside the pillar to save Prahlada,[1] can appear in any place or form

---

1 A staunch devotee of Lord Vishnu. Though constantly persecuted by his demonic father, Hiranyakashipu, Prahlada's unwavering faith in the omnipresence of the Lord saved him from all trials and tribulations. Once, in response to his father's sarcastic question, "Does your Lord dwell in this

to a devotee who has total surrender, because it is not circumscribed by space or time. Nor does it require a particular medium for its manifestation. If there is a divine resolve, even animals will chant Vedic mantras.

The life of saint Jnanadeva of Alandi, Pune District, Maharashtra is an example of this. Though born into a Brahmin family, Jnanadeva and his siblings were denied the social status of Brahmins because his father gave up a renunciate's life, got married and became a householder. His four children, therefore, were not permitted to learn the Vedas or other scriptures. The authorities turned a deaf ear to their appeals to reinstate their social status. Jnanadeva said that their knowledge was nothing, that he could even make a bull chant the Vedas. He then commanded a bull standing nearby to recite the Vedas and to everyone's wonderment, the bull began to chant the Vedas…! There is another story of him instructing a ma-

---

pillar, too?" Prahlada coolly answered in the affirmative, provoking his father to strike the pillar with his sword. From the pillar emerged Narasimha, the half-man-half-lion incarnation of Lord Vishnu, who killed Hiranyakashipu.

sonry wall to move and the wall listened 'to his master's order' and moved.

These are some of the amazing stories of the sages who lived in the past. However, here and now, one can personally see and experience every moment as the enactment of the infinite power and grandeur of God's resolve in Amma's holy presence.

# 2 | EPITOME OF VEDANTA

After receiving Amma's darshan, people tell me, "When I went near Amma, my mind became blank. All questions vanished. I couldn't say anything I wanted to say." There are also people who say, "When Amma held me, I started crying. I couldn't utter a word. I wonder if Amma understood my problems." Yet, there are others who say, "I felt so peaceful and happy in Amma's presence that I was in a totally absorbed state. I have never experienced such love." Then there are people who completely open up in Amma's presence. They just unburden all their anxieties, fears, anger and other negativities to her, helping them feel relieved and relaxed.

All over the world, when people come for Amma's darshan, they are likely to have one of these experiences. Why is it that we cry or become silent before Amma? Why do we feel so happy and peaceful in her presence? What inspires us to share all our emotions when we are with Amma? The answer is – Amma's pure undivided love.

Amma's embrace is the touch of boundless love. Our contact with that purity, will open up

what is already inside of us. It is the same principle as magnetizing an iron rod. When we keep rubbing an iron rod with a magnet, the rod will soon become magnetized. Similarly, the presence of unlimited love revives the slumbering love in us. This may still give only a glimpse of the vast expansiveness of love, but once we relish that, the desire to experience it more and more will arise and gradually intensify.

Reporters ask Amma, "Do you think a mere hug can transform people?" She responds, "This is not a mere physical embrace. It is a true meeting, a meeting of hearts. I flow to them, and they flow to me."

Journalists also ask, "You sit and hug people for hours on end? Who hugs you?" Her answer is, "The entire creation hugs me. We are in an eternal embrace. It is the touch of this totality of love's pure energy that creates the transformation."

Amma's pure and selfless love serves as a striking contrast between what true love is, and the love we see in the world. This contrast can be used as an effective tool to rise above the lower feelings of love. In matters of life and love, Amma's love helps us differentiate between quality and quantity.

We live in the world not as we truly are, but as an identity we gain from our name, power, position, educational qualification, etc. We are also known to others by those identities, such as a police officer, government official, politician, artist, and CEO. Like this, throughout life, we live as someone else. The question is, am I just these roles that I identify with and society has attributed to me, or do I have another identity? Who am I?

Whether we accept it or not, from a spiritual point of view, human beings do have an identity crisis. We cover it up with all that we acquire throughout life. Eventually, we lose track and identify with whatever we have stockpiled, remaining inside the cocoon and regarding that as our real abode. The mask has been such an integral part of our life. We have worn the mask for so long that now we mistake the mask for our real face, while the original face is hidden behind.

When Sri Shankara, the exponent of *Advaita* (non-dual) philosophy, met his guru Govinda Bhagavatpada, he asked Shankara, "Who are you?"

Shankara immediately responded to the question with a Sanskrit verse, composed extemporaneously, which later came to be known as *Atma Shatkam*, or *Nirvana Shatkam*:

> *manō buddhyahankāra cittāni nāham*
> *na ca śrotrajihvē na ca ghrāṇa nētrē*
> *na ca vyōma bhūmir na tējō na vāyuḥ*
> *cidānanda rūpaḥ śivō'ham śivō'ham*

> I am not the mind, nor intelligence, nor the ego, nor the faculty of recollections. I am not the faculties of hearing, nor that of tasting, the faculties of smelling or seeing. I am not the sky, nor the earth, nor the fire or the air. I am the ever-pure, blissful consciousness; I am Shiva, I am Shiva, the ever-pure blissful consciousness.

I recall an incident from the early 80's. There was a man in the village who severely abused and criticized Amma. One day, Amma was coming back to the ashram after a house visit when Amma saw this man at the ashram boat jetty, waiting for the boat to cross the backwaters. As we disembarked the boat that he was about to climb into, it was obvious that he had a serious infection on both his arms, as they were full of pus and blood. Without even thinking for a moment, Amma went up to him and lovingly enquired about the wounds, caressed his arms and even kissed them as she wished him well and took leave of him. Tears welled up in the man's eyes, and he became overwhelmed with emotion.

We needn't look so far back as the early days to find an example of Amma's state of being. Just walk into one of the venues where Amma is giving darshan and watch her for just a few minutes.

During Europe tour (2018), Amma fractured her right little toe. As Dr. Priya was the physician on the tour, she made a big deal of this and tried many tactics to immobilize Amma's toe. While she was trying one of the many contraptions, Amma pulled her foot away and told Dr. Priya that she didn't want any immobilization.

Priya argued back saying, "Amma! You will have a lot of pain… I am telling you…" Amma glared at her and said with a sarcastic look, "Pain? I decide when I experience pain… you cannot tell me when I will and will not feel pain." These were not mere words. Amma continued to give darshan for more than 16 hours each day with the fractured toe! Medically it is inexplicable… These are just a few of the innumerable occasions on which Amma has clearly shown that her happiness does not need to depend on her external environment, or even the body.

In the case of most great spiritual masters, or people who served society selflessly, who really created a change and influenced minds across the globe, stories about them go something like this:

"Once upon a time there was a beautiful blue complexioned boy in Vrindavan named Krishna. However…

"Once upon a time there was a young prince named Rama, who was going to be crowned King. However…"

"Once upon a time, there was a prince named Siddharth, who later became Buddha. However…

"Once upon a time, there was a young wise man named Jesus of Nazareth, son of Mary and Joseph. However…"

"Once upon a time, there was a young girl named Sudhamani, who was very compassionate and who had an intense desire to realize God. However…"

What do all these stories — and all stories for that matter — have in common? They begin with life going smoothly, but we all know what is coming. What is coming is the word "however." The word "however" is always looming. It comes in every story. In fact, it is actually what makes the story interesting. It is the conflict. Without the "however," there is no story.

Amma's life is full of "howevers." But for Amma, the "howevers" are not "howevers" at all. They are simply "events." They don't cause any bump in the flow of her life or in the change that she seeks to create in the world.

Fearlessness is one of the signs of a perfect guru. As long as you are identified with your achievements in the world, as a mere physical entity, in forgetfulness of your true identity, fearlessness will not arise. We are constantly being haunted by all sorts of fear. We exist in fear. Even our love is gripped by fear. To eliminate this fear, we must embark on another journey, the journey from the body to the soul. That journey, if completed successfully, will end in total fearlessness. Even fear of death disappears.

There is a beautiful verse by a 14th century poetess-saint from Kashmir, named Lalleshwari, that epitomizes the attitude one with true spiritual attainment has towards death.

> O Infinite Consciousness,
> brimming with elixir,
> You live within my body,
> and I worship only You.
> I do not care
> if I die, take birth,
> or pass into some other state.
> These things are so ordinary now.

The saints and sages tell us that heaven is not something that one should long to reach after death. Heaven is not some luxury beachside resort that exists high up, where comforts and pleasures are available round the clock, seven days a week, 365 days a year. It is not a concept but, instead, a reality that can be experienced here, while living in this world. It is a permanent state of even-mindedness and equanimity that will destroy every trace of fear. Once established in that height of consciousness, you will forever remain in perfect peace and bliss. Even in the death of the body, you are in bliss. Just like any other event, death also becomes one more event. You can celebrate it wholeheartedly.

A mahatma once was asked, "Holy one, are you sure that you will go to heaven when you die?"

The mahatma replied, "Yes, of course."

"But how do you know?" the man asked. "You are not dead, and you don't even know what is in God's mind."

The mahatma replied, "Look here. It is true that I have no idea what is in God's mind, but I know my mind. I am always full of peace and bliss wherever I am, even if I'm in hell itself."

There is no doubt in my mind that Amma is absolutely fearless. I have never seen her afraid. Never. She is so established in the unchangeable substratum, that there is not even a trace of fear.

In 2002, Amma had a program scheduled in Gujarat during a time when it was full of rioting. All the government officials, as well as the devotees, pleaded with Amma not to go. But Amma calmly said, "Those who are afraid to die need not come. I'm going."

I remember another incident where Amma showed the same fearlessness. During the 2004

Indian Ocean tsunami, Amma charged right down into the floodwaters. Another wave could have come at any moment, but Amma was not the least bit concerned about herself. She was only concerned about her children.

Amma not only possesses *jnana* (true knowledge), she is a *jnananishtha* (firmly established knowledge.) She is what Krishna refers to in the Gita as *sthitaprajna* (a person who abides in the exalted state of pure awareness.) And this is the source of her fearlessness. Her focus is not on the changing phenomena but on the changeless substratum. And that makes her invincible.

Amma embodies the following two verses of the *Bhagavad Gita*:

> *nainam chindanti śastrāṇi nainam dahati pāvakaḥ*
> *na cainam klēdayantyāpo na śoṣayati mārutaḥ*
> *acchēdyō'yam adāhyo'yam aklēdyō'śoṣya eva ca*
> *nityaḥ sarva-gataḥ sthāṇur acalō'yam sanātanaḥ*

Weapons cannot shred the soul, nor can fire burn it. Water cannot wet it, nor can the wind dry it. The soul is unbreakable and incombustible; it can neither be dampened nor dried. It is everlasting, in all places, unalterable, immutable, and primordial. (23 - 24)

As you know, when Amma holds a program, tens of thousands of people come. Everyone is admitted. No one is turned away. And I'll be honest... Sometimes, people who are mentally unstable, even insane, come for Amma's darshan. If 10,000 people come, there may be 10 or so that are relatively unbalanced. And some of these people... let's just say that, if you were walking down the street and they were coming your direction, surely you would cross over to the other side of the road. Some of these people come on their own; others are brought by their families. Some are so disturbed that they are screaming and flailing their arms. Sometimes, in India, the devotees and disciples assisting Amma's darshan have to hold the arms of these people tightly, so that they don't strike Amma when she blesses them. Their insanity is so intense it is as if they were possessed by demons. And I'll admit, the devotees and disciples assisting with Amma's darshan often become a bit nervous because these people could do anything. They are not in control of themselves. They could bite you, hit you, or even strangle you to death.

But I would bet my life that if you were to monitor Amma's heartbeat during such incidents, you would find that it doesn't increase even one beat per minute. This is jnananistha. She knows through and through that only the body can be harmed and that she is not the body, but the Self.

You may have heard the legendary story of King Theseus. Supposedly, King Theseus founded the city of Athens, the capital of Greece. Apparently, the King fought many battles. Hence, the citizens of Athens dedicated a memorial in his honor, where they preserved his ship. It is believed that the ship stayed there for hundreds of years, but as the years went by, some planks of the ship started to decay. In order to keep the ship looking nice, the rotting planks were replaced with brand new planks of the same material.

The question is, will the ship be the same if people of each generation keep changing each rotting plank? Suppose there were 1,000 planks, and what if 999 of them were replaced? Is that one plank, yet to be replaced, enough to keep the ship's originality? This is an eternal philosophical question, known as the 'problem of identity.'

Even though the scientific world is still debating about the exact number of cells in a human body, roughly, the body of an average human being contains around 30 to 40 trillion cells. It still remains a mystery to be precise.

Our ancient *rishis*[2] foresaw these subtle changes thousands of years ago. They identified this ever-changing principle of the universe, not just the human body, but all external appearances. They also realized the ultimate principle, the truth that remains unchanged.

According to medical researchers at Stanford and other reputable universities of the world, except for certain cells that are never replaced, the body is replaced with a largely new set of cells every 7 years to 10 years. Some of our most

---

2 Seers, i.e. spiritually enlightened individuals who intuitively perceived the sacred mantras that encapsulate Vedic wisdom.

important parts are revamped even more rapidly. Can you imagine?

If every living and non-living thing is in a constant flux, what is this physical body? I am referring to the bodies of all living beings. If change is a truth, how do we remain the same? Objectively speaking, there is no correct answer, because within a span of seven years, virtually every single cell of our body dies and new ones are generated. So, plainly speaking, as we grow older, you and I are not the same person. In that case, what is our true identity?

Thousands of years before the story of Theseus, the sages of India gave us a technique known as 'neti neti' which means the 'method of negation.' The ultimate truth, Brahman, is not an object. It is the one and only subject. It is neither the seen (which is the object) nor is it the process of seeing. It is the seer, the subject (the I in you). You are not a name and various other modifications attributed to that. You are the truth.

The *Brhadaranyaka Upanishad* says:

> nēti nēti, na hyētasmāditi
> nētyanyatparamasti; atha
> nāmadheyam—satyasya satyamiti; prāṇā

*vai satyam, teṣāmeṣa satyam ǁ 3 ǁ iti*
*tṛtīyam brāhmaṇam ǁ*

Now, therefore, the description (of
Brahman): 'Not this, not this.' Because
there is no other and more appropriate
description than this: 'Not this.' Now
Its name: 'The Truth of truth.' The vital
force is truth, and It is the Truth of that.
(2.3.6)

A close observation of Amma's life will reveal
that she is pure Vedanta in action. Nothing is
insignificant or inessential for her. Even the so-
called unimportant things have a meaning, have a
place in life, because for Amma everything is the
'essence.' "Nothing is insignificant or unimportant
in life," says Amma.

There are big and small trees. We have big
lotus flowers and small roadside flowers. Some
flowers have a sweet fragrance, and others have
an unpleasant odor. The majestic looking peacock
with its plume widespread and the black complexioned crow coexist here. While the cuckoo sings
melodiously, the little sparrow also sings in its own
way. The presence of even a tiny creature is also

significant. The world and the creation would be incomplete without this being so. We should not compare. Value everything.

Hence, Amma doesn't dismiss the grievances and weaknesses of ordinary people, calling them 'unreal' or 'illusory.' Her way is that of understanding an individual's level of maturity, listening with utmost empathy, giving practical advice, offering what she can to make them feel happy and peaceful, and gradually helping them understand spiritual principles. Amma is the epitome of Vedanta in every sense.

Visualize this. You are standing by the side of a road, watching all the different vehicles passing by: the buses… trucks… cars of various makes and models… limousines… ambulances… perhaps, even a hearse… You are standing there for a while and simply taking in all those different vehicles passing by. Then shift your focus to the road. The road is constant. The road is permanent. The road is the substratum upon which all the phenomena is constantly changing. Even in the heaviest traffic—even in so-called "bumper-to-bumper" traffic—there will be some small space, some gap, through which we can see the substratum. If we want to become fearless, this is all we need to do. We need to shift our attention from the changing to the changeless—from the objects to the substratum. This is what Amma does. Slowly she will help us shift our attention from the objects to the substratum.

# 3 | CALL AND RESPONSE

The story of Sabari, in the *Ramayana*, is known to almost everyone. She was a tribal woman and the daughter of a hunter. Sabari used to serve sage Matanga, whom she considered her guru, with freshly picked fruits from the forest. Pleased by her devotion and selflessness, the sage, just before he left his body, told Sabari that one day Lord Rama will visit the ashram and bless her.

Sabari took the sage's words to heart. From that day onwards, Sabari, with unwavering faith,

waited for the Lord's arrival. With great anticipation, she would sweep several kilometers of the
pathway every single day. She walked through the
forest and removed thorns, stones and drooping
vines, for she thought that the creepers would get
caught in Rama's uncombed hair. She broke the
lumps of earth, as she didn't want Rama's soft feet
to get hurt from them. She also collected fresh
fruits for the Lord to eat. Sabari had no idea what
Rama looked like, but unflinching was her faith,
absolute was her devotion and flawless was her love
for the Lord. Thirteen long years passed by like
this. Sabari waited for her Lord, day in and day
out. One day, Rama came along with his brother
Lakshmana. The moment Sabari saw Rama, she
knew it was her Lord, even though she was unfamiliar with Rama's appearance. The pure bliss
she experienced when she saw Rama was enough
for her to recognize the Lord.

Sabari washed the Lord's feet and offered fruits
for him to eat. Because she wanted to give the
sweetest among the fruits to Rama, Sabari first
took a bite herself, tasting each fruit before giving
it to the Lord. Sabari also wanted to ensure that
the fruits she gave to Rama weren't poisonous.

The Lord said, "Mother, just as your heart, these fruits are also very sweet, the sweetest I ever had."

In the *Bhagavad Gita*, Lord Krishna says:

> *patram puṣpam phalam tōyam yō mē*
> *bhaktyā prayacchati*
> *tadaham bhaktyupahṛtam aśnāmi*
> *prayatātmanaḥ*

> Whoever offers Me with devotion, a leaf, a flower, a fruit or water, I accept that, the pious offering of the pure in heart. (9.26)

The *Ramayana* says that even though there were other saints waiting to welcome Lord Rama to their ashram, He only visited Sabari. This was solely owing to her selfless and pure devotion to the Lord. According to the scripture, Sabari, herself, put this question to Lord Rama, "There were many spiritually accomplished yogis waiting for your darshan, but you came to this worthless devotee's hermitage. Oh Lord, to you, only pure devotion matters, neither knowledge, caste, creed, nor color."

Rama was immensely pleased by Sabari's love and devotion. Before he left, Rama told Sabari, "Ask for anything. I will fulfill your wish."

Sabari said, "Lord, after having your darshan, what more do I need? I have no more desires. For what shall I live now? I lived only to see you. My Lord, now my one and only wish is to merge in you." Sabari attained liberation immediately and left her body soon after that.

Sabari was low-caste, illiterate and had no knowledge of the scriptures. Yet, her unshakeable faith in the guru's words, her steadfastness and innocent devotion, took her to the highest peak of human existence.

To quote the *Bhakti Sutras* of sage Narada:

> *nāsti tēṣu jāti-vidyā-rūpa-kula-dhana-kriyādi-bhedaḥ*

> Amongst them there exists no distinctions of caste, learning, beauty, lineage, riches, observances and the like. (72)

I recall Amma's words, "Unlike other paths, the path of devotion helps one enjoy its fruits from the very beginning. This is because other paths have certain rules and regulations that the practitioner must follow strictly. Some paths have a certain degree of logical thinking and analysis involved. Only if you adhere to those conventions will you obtain the results. Conversely, the path of devotion has no such rules. The one and only qualification it demands is love, which is natural to everyone. Just love God with all your heart, period. Have you seen a jackfruit tree? Unlike normal fruit trees, a jackfruit tree bears fruit even at the base of the tree. The path of devotion is like that. You will experience the result right away."

If you take a closer look at Sabari's story from the *Ramayana*, we will find Sabari's three main qualities: pure love, *prema*; unceasing hope, *pratiksha*; and endless patience, *kshama*. In other words, one needs love endowed with hope and patience to qualify as a true devotee of the Lord.

Sabari waited thirteen long years in anticipation, and by the time the Lord arrived, Sabari was old and fragile. Yet, she never gave up or compromised on her love, faith, hope and patience.

Genuine devotees will not be satisfied with anything else, until they are able to see their Lord in all of creation.

The *Isavasya Upanishad* says:

> *hiraṇmayena pātreṇa*
> *satyasyāpihitam mukham*
> *tat tvam pūṣann apāvṛṇu*

*satya-dharmāya dṛṣṭaye*

The seeker of truth supplicates, "O Sun (Truth), please remove the gold cover concealing Your face. Allow Your devotee to see Your face hidden behind the concealment." (15)

What is this 'gold cover?' It is all that one gains or tries to gain in the material world: power, fame, wealth and so forth. The seeker of truth says, 'I am not interested in any of those things. My one and only prayer is to see the reality behind the covering.'

Ordinarily, when people see someone flourishing in the world, they believe that God is so merciful to them, but not in the eyes of a true spiritual aspirant, a fully surrendered devotee. The devotee doesn't consider riches and worldly achievements God's blessing but, instead, as a hindrance on his path. So, the rishi says, 'Please don't be kind to me by showering material prosperity on me. That is not the kind of benevolence I wish to have from You. I have no craving for this so-called wealth. Reveal Your reality. That alone will make me happy.' The verse can also mean,

'I am not interested in nourishing the body and mind, the container, the outer cover. Remove all my attachments, so that I can experience my real nature, the indwelling Self.'

The sun's rays are so powerful, immensely brilliant, that it is extremely difficult for us to look straight at it. The sun's rays act like a screen, a veil that blocks us from viewing the sun. Likewise, we are not able to see the truth because of its brilliance. Hence, the prayer is, "Help me go beyond that, so that I can have a direct experience of you."

What ordinary people consider to be wealth is insignificant for a true devotee. Amma tells a beautiful story of a thief who broke into the houses of the *gopis* (milkmaids) in Vrindavan. He thought he stole all their valuables because they were all wrapped in exquisite and expensive clothes.

However, as the thief began to untie the 'precious loot' that was carefully covered with layers of clothes, what he found inside totally disappointed him. In each of the bundles, he could only find a torn piece of yellow silk, an old worn out peacock feather, a dried sliver of sandal paste, a dried tulasi garland, a half empty container of *kumkum* (saffron powder), a single bell from an anklet, a broken piece of a bracelet, a small conch, a piece of a broken mud pot, etc. — all worthless items!

The thief was frustrated as well as surprised. Why on earth had these gopis kept such worthless items so safely tucked in their vaults? What makes these items so valuable to them? At the risk of being punished for stealing, the thief was overwhelmed with curiosity to know the truth. He took all the items with him and went back to Vrindavan.

When the thief returned all the stolen items, the gopis were so full of bliss. Unable to contain their joy, they jumped and danced, as if they suddenly owned the whole world. Not only that, they also removed all their gold ornaments and gave them to the thief as a token of their gratitude for returning the 'worthless things.' The thief was flabbergasted. He couldn't understand what was happening.

Once the excitement settled down a little bit, he asked the gopis, "May I know why these petty things are so valuable to you?"

The gopis explained, "Our most beloved Krishna used these items a long time back, when he was here in Vrindavan with us. This peacock feather was worn by him. That piece of pot was one that he broke to steal butter from a gopi's house. This yellow silk cloth was what he was wearing on the day he stole butter from my house, and when I tried to grab him, that little torn piece of cloth was all that I could manage to get hold of! Whenever we look at them, each of these pieces brings us the overwhelming joy of the days we had spent in the company of Krishna! It's these precious mementos that give some joy to us amidst our life filled with the sorrow of separation from our beloved Krishna."

The thief couldn't hold back his tears as he witnessed the pure innocent love of the gopis. His heart melted. He gave back all the gold jewelry, so generously gifted by the gopis. A life of stealing was no longer attractive to him. He had an intense desire to see Krishna. He came to know from the gopis that Krishna was in Mathura. The thief immediately left for Mathura. There, he saw the most enchanting form of Krishna for the first time. With tears of bliss streaming down his face, the thief prostrated at Krishna's holy feet.

With a mischievous smile, the all-knowing Lord gazed at the thief and said, "One thief is enough for Vrindavan!" The thief, however, was totally absorbed in Krishna's divine beauty.

Narrating the glory of a true devotee, sage Narada, in his aphorisms of devotion, says:

> *kantha-avarōdha-rōmañca-aśrubhiḥ*
> *parasparam lapa-mānāḥ pāvayanti kulāni*
> *pṛthivīm ca.*

> Such devotees conversing together with a choking voice, with hairs standing on end, and with tears flowing, purify their families as well as the earth. (68)

The bond between the Lord and his devotee, the guru and the disciple, are beyond the intellect and logic. It is a deep feeling of oneness, an identity. Someone who has not experienced such love, who has only known love as a physiological relationship between two people, may not understand the depth and purity of that love. They will surely misinterpret it, perhaps even brand it as craziness. Obviously, there is some degree of craziness even in ordinary love (worldly love). "I am madly in love with you," is a common phrase used throughout the world. If that is the case, the 'madness' in spiritual love, which is beyond physiological and emotional love, is much greater, because love, whether spiritual or worldly, is irrational. Logic and rationalization have no place in love.

As Amma says, "Love never gets old. It is ever new."

Objects and people become old, less useful and less attractive. The older they grow, the less the attraction and joy. But real love's beauty and attraction are everlasting. People say, "The love I had for my partner diminished." Impartial self-introspection will reveal that they never had any love for that person in the first place. What was interpreted as 'love' was just a physical and emotional attraction. Worldly love always remains at that level, never penetrating beyond.

In Amma's own words, "Love is a constant feeling. Irrespective of time and place, it always remains within you. No one tells their beloved, 'Okay, tomorrow from 2:00 p.m. to 3:00 p.m. is the time to express love…!' It is unheard of."

Love is a mysterious thing. The more you try to explain it, the more mysterious it becomes.

Recently, I was talking to a young surgeon who was describing the complicated surgical procedures he does. He concluded by saying, "You know, Swamiji, as our scriptures say, the body is such a miserable and disgusting thing. It is just filth." Just a few moments after making this statement, the doctor switched his conversation to his girlfriend and how he couldn't convince his parents that he should marry this girl. He became emotional and told me, "But I can't live without her."

Do you see the obvious contradiction in the doctor's attitude? First, he remarked about the repulsive nature of the human body. The next moment he was talking about his beloved with so much excitement and emotion. What does this mean? It means love is something beyond the body. In reality, it doesn't see the body, its limitations, the dirt, ugliness and all the petty feelings. Love, whether it is ordinary or spiritual, transcends the human intellect and all its calculations.

There is no way to measure love. One can only observe or sense the identification that one has for his lover. The more you are identified with your lover, the more love you have. For example, what would be your answer if someone asked you,

"Whom do you love the most, your work or your wife?" Your spontaneous answer, the response you give even without thinking for a moment, reveals the degree of your love. The answer, whatever it is, discloses the strength of your identification.

Depending on the identification, you also develop a oneness with your lover. In such a relationship, communication happens even without the medium of words. This phenomenon happens even in ordinary love. We hear of so many incidents where lovers say, "I just thought about talking to her and she called me… I had a dream of him introducing his parents to me, and I was totally surprised when he actually introduced his parents to me the very next day. I hadn't even told him about the dream."

If this happens even in ordinary love, a feeling or sensation based on the physical and emotional planes of consciousness, then spiritual love, an experience beyond the realms of the body and mind, will certainly unite the devotee with the Lord and the disciple with his guru in a much deeper way. That communion has a considerably greater 'call and response' dimension to it, as well.

From the countless experiences Amma has graciously showered on me, I would like to share one incident to show the power of 'call and response.'

In 1981, when Amma asked me to take a master's degree in Philosophy, I asked Amma, "Who will teach me?" Amma said, "There is a professor in Changanassery (a town about 50 kilometers away from the ashram). Go talk to him, and he will come here to teach you." I went in search of this professor, whom I had never met before. I had no idea whether he would be willing to come to the ashram and teach me, but had full trust in Amma's words. I found out that the professor was an eminent scholar, having authored more than 25 books. In the mid 1970's, he had gone to the United States as a Fulbright Scholar for his higher studies in western philosophy.

I went to his house first. His wife told me that he was at the college, so I went there. As I was waiting to see him, I imagined a serious looking, highly mature person, wearing a modern outfit to appear in front of me at any moment. I was a little nervous, as I had never met him before and had no idea of his nature.

After I waited for half an hour in a classroom, a funny looking person walked into the room. At first I thought it was some random person, but was bowled over when he introduced himself as the professor I was waiting to see. I don't want to be disrespectful, but to be frank, he looked like a much funnier Indian version of Hardy, of the famous Laurel and Hardy comedy duo. His lips were reddish from the betel leaves, tobacco and areca nut combination (*paan*) he had been chewing. The professor's mouth was so full with that stuff that he could hardly speak. With a turban tied around his head, his *dhoti* folded up, and his rolling big eyes, I thought to myself, "What a bizarre figure! Forget it. He will never come to teach me. Even if he does come, how am I going to sit in front of this weird-looking person and learn? I have to ask Amma to find someone else."

Even though his presence made me feel very uncomfortable, I introduced myself and explained the purpose of my visit. His immediate response was, "I cannot come there. I will not. I have no time. If you want, come here on weekends. I will try to find some time for you." Then he added,

"Also, I am an atheist. I have absolutely no desire to spend time in an ashram atmosphere."

The chapter was closed then and there. He got up from his seat and walked towards the door. Not being able to convince him to come to the ashram to teach me, I was about to leave as well. As I turned to leave the classroom, I heard a voice from behind.

"One moment…" It was the professor again. He continued, "Somehow, I am unable to say, 'no' to you by looking at your face. So, I will come next weekend to your place to check out the environment." I suddenly knew it was Amma's work.

As intellectual people can sometimes be, this professor was a little eccentric. On certain days, he would begin the class before I arrived even though I was his one and only student.

Once, just a couple of weekends after he started coming to the ashram, I entered into a heated argument with him. On those days, we only had small huts to stay in. Amma was giving darshan in one of those huts at the farthest end of the property, while the professor and I were sitting on the other end, where Amma's parents stayed. Just before the class began, I turned around facing

Amma's picture and prayed. As soon I finished praying, the professor made a comment, "Why do you pray? Is she going to hear your prayers? Your hard work is everything. Other than that, no God or guru will come to help you."

I was deeply hurt by his comment. I felt as if someone had questioned my faith in Amma and the ancient guru-disciple relationship as a whole. Of course, it is not my job to go around convincing people about my path and faith. It is not necessary. However, on the spur of the moment, I firmly responded to the professor. "Yes, Amma hears every single prayer. Do you want to see?"

He said, "Yes, if you dare."

With all my heart, I told the professor in a stern voice, "You just watch and see. We are far away from the hut where Amma is giving darshan, and I am sitting here with you. But, you just watch, within the next few moments, Amma will send someone to call me."

He said, "Okay, let's see. I am sure it is not going to happen."

I said, "Amma is definitely going to call me. Once that happens, will you come and bow down to her?" By then, it was almost four weekends since the professor had started his classes. Even so, he hadn't so much as greeted Amma even once. He was pretty confident that Amma wouldn't call me within the next couple of minutes, as he had never seen that happening in the middle of the class so far.

From a logical and circumstantial point of view, a sudden and unexpected call from Amma was not supposed to happen. In those day, there were no such urgent things. So, the professor said, "Yes, 100% I will. I give you my word." But, the universe's decisions are unpredictable.

Just a couple of minutes later, a brahmachari appeared in front of the door of the hut and told me, "Amma is calling you."

As the professor sat there with his eyes popping out, I ran out of the hut to see Amma. When I reached there, Amma looked at me and asked me only one question, "Son, did you call Amma?"

I had no words to express my inner feeling. As I stood gazing at her with a heart full of love and gratitude, I saw the professor enter the darshan hut and fall at Amma's Feet.

That is the power of real prayer.

Amma says, "God always listens to our prayers. However, we only have the right to pray. When to respond is God's decision. It is in God's hands. Human rules of call and response are not applicable. One should have the strong faith that whether God responds now or later, or in another birth, it is for our best. Sometimes God responds immediately. If so, remember that it is to deepen our faith. A delayed response, after waiting for a long period, means God wants us to deepen our faith. And, if there is no response at all, then realize that God has something divine in store for us."

The guru's whole purpose is to show the disciple that in reality the guru and disciple are one—that they both are of the same consciousness. The disciple's heart is closed, blocked with layers of negativities accumulated through countless births. The thoughts and emotions in his mind create a bumper-to-bumper traffic congestion. The guru knows every technique to clear the unceasing traffic. She also knows all kinds of short-cuts you can take to reach the destination faster as she is the only one who is familiar with the right keys to open the heart. Once the heart is open, the guru with a feather touch, will push the disciple into the vast ocean of *sat-chit-ananda* (pure being, pure consciousness and pure bliss). The heart is the gateway to God and Self-realization.

It is not easy to reach that 'opening point of the heart.' The culprit is the mind. At present, the mind, with its innumerable doubts and deep-seated habits, has fully overtaken and overpowered the heart. It is difficult to convince the mind of anything.

The mind accumulates everything, both good and bad, necessary and unnecessary. I had a friend who had an urge to touch all the parked vehicles he passed on the road as he was walking. No matter whether we, his friends, were with him, or people were watching him, he would stick to his strange habit. We used to tease him for acting in this weird manner, but he would say, "I cannot help it. I just have to do it." The human mind functions in a similar manner. It wants to 'touch' every random thing, whether or not it makes sense.

Judgmental as we are, most of the time we can't even act logically. Let me give you an example. Many people have important questions to ask Amma, including making major decisions in their life. The thing is, they might have already mentally decided their course of action. They only expect Amma to agree with their decision…! If not, they think Amma hasn't given them the right guidance. This is a wrong attitude, devoid of devotion, love and faith. You are only looking for validation of the decisions you already made. You have reversed the whole order of it.

If you are so confident about your decision-making capacities, why seek Amma's advice in the first place? Go ahead and do as you wish, praying for the guru's blessings. Don't blame God or the guru. Or, be open, take the guru's guidance and act accordingly.

A Satguru such as Amma is like our most trustworthy friend. She holds our hand and takes us on the right path, helps us to open our eyes, helps us to transcend the mind. That's when our third eye opens, when we start looking inwards.

The Upanishads offer us so many examples of genuine *guru-bhakti* (devotion to the guru). There are many stories of disciples who became enlightened simply due to their devotion, obedience, selflessness and surrender to the guru. Such guru-bhakti works like electricity passing from one end of an electric cable to the other, from the guru to the disciple.

The transcendental experience of the ancient rishis, as conveyed in the scriptures, gives us strong indications of a supreme reality, a cosmic intelligence. However, as far as disciples and devotees are concerned, God is just a concept, an image they see in a temple or in pictures.

Yet, all these concepts described in the scriptures take shape in a Satguru. The Satguru is the embodiment of love, compassion, purity, patience, forbearance, perseverance, subtlety and all other noble qualities. They are the only proof of the existence of God, the supreme reality. The Satguru's presence, words and actions unmistakably declare, "Yes, God is, because the guru is."

Hence the *Guru Gita* says:

> *dhyānamūlam gurōrmūrtiḥ pūjāmūlam*
> *gurōḥ padam*
> *mantramūlam gurōrvākyam mōkṣamūlam*
> *gurōḥ kṛpā*

The root of meditation is the guru's form; the root of worship is the guru's feet; the root of mantra is the guru's word; the root of liberation is the guru's Grace. (1 - 2)

# 4 | THE DIVINE MUSIC THAT WOKE ME UP

When we hear the melody of the bamboo flute, the first thing that comes to mind is the form of Muralidharan,[3] Lord Krishna, who always played divine music on his flute. The music emerging from his bamboo flute was so enchanting and melodious, it even attracted birds, animals and celestial beings.

*Murali* (flute) and Muralidharan[1] are akin to the relationship between the devotee and the

---

3 Bearer of the flute; another name of Lord Krishna.

Lord. But for me, Krishna did not live only in Vrindavan and Mathura. He was not just the son of Devaki and Vasudeva. He was not only in Dvaapara Yuga;[4] nor was he only in Dwarakapuri. He is right here, now, with me, living in this world. He just changed his physical appearance from a male form to a female and is also known by a new name, Amma, Sri Mata Amritanandamayi Devi. The dwelling place also has changed from Dwarakapuri to Amritapuri.

You may feel disappointed if you want to see the same Krishna who lived five thousand years ago, who took birth in Mathura and was brought to Vrindavan where he sported with the *gopas* (cowherd boys) and gopis, a peacock feather tucked in his hairlocks, playing the bamboo flute, who became the charioteer of the great warrior Arjuna, the third Pandava brother in the Mahabharata War, and who gave the most profound teaching, known as the *Bhagavad Gita*. Why will you feel disappointed? Because God is infinity

4 One of the four yugas (ages) that, according to Hindu cosmology, characterize one cycle of creation. Lord Krishna lived during the Dvapara Yuga and was the ruler of the Dwaraka kingdom. The present age is known as the Kali Yuga.

and God doesn't repeat. God does not assume the same form again. Only human beings with limited resources do things repeatedly, but they may feel bored. God, being infinite, assumes infinite names and forms. There is no boredom. There is only expansiveness.

Krishna was a beautiful and impeccable blend of the cosmic feminine and masculine energies, the creator and creatrix aspects in perfect balance. So, too, is Amma.

What about the flute playing, one may wonder? That question is to be expected. What issued from the bamboo flute of Lord Krishna wasn't just music; it was the imperishable melody of supreme love, drawing all creatures, moving and unmoving, unto him. Amma's bhajans do the same. One cannot listen to Amma's bhajans without being inextricably drawn to her.

The word 'krshnaha' is derived from the Sanskrit root 'krsh.' It means, variously, to attract, to plough and to uproot. These terms sprout wings in Amma's presence. Amma is pure love, which draws hearts to surrender to her. She is the Satguru who ploughs the fields of our minds, purifies us by smashing to smithereens the stones and lumps of impurities therein, sows the seeds of noble virtues within, and helps us gradually attain the fruit of Self-realization. If you look at it that way, you will see that Lord Krishna and the music of his divine flute, and Amma's hallowed presence, which is the source of boundless love, are one. Amma is the sacred song of supreme love that touches and awakens the divine in humanity.

Self-realized souls are one with the formless transcendental reality. In order for them to assume a form and work in the world, they need to make a special sankalpa. That sankalpa can only be explained as their pure love and compassion for humanity. However, even while engaged in the divine mission they have to accomplish, they are fully detached and untouched by both the actions and the results. Perfectly established in the state of sahaja samadhi, they have no sense of 'I' and 'mine.' Even in the midst of all activities, they are totally free from ego and ever content.

The *Mundaka Upanishad* depicts this beautifully:

> *dvā suparṇā sayujā sakhāyā samānam*
> *vṛkṣam pariṣasvajātē*

*tayōr anyaḥ pippalam svadu atti anaśnan*
*anyō abhicākaśīti*
*samāne vṛkṣē puruṣō nimagno anīśayā*
*śōcati muhyamānaḥ*
*juṣṭam yadā paśyati anyam īśam asya*
*mahimānam iti vītaśōkaḥ*

Like two birds of golden plumage,
inseparable companions, are perched on
a branch of the same tree. One of them
tastes the sweet and bitter fruits of the
tree; the other, tasting neither, calmly
looks on. On the same tree, the individual
self (*jiva*), deluded by forgetfulness of his
identity with the divine Self, bewildered
by his ego, grieves and is sad. But when
he recognizes the other as the Lord
worshipped by all and His glory, he
becomes free from grief. (3.1.1 - 2)

Here, in this world of diversity, God and human
beings, all living beings for that matter exist together. In reality, existence is impossible without
God. So, 'I exist' means, 'I am only because God
is.' This awareness frees one of all forms of grief,
such as sadness, anxiety, depression, anger, greed,

jealousy, hatred, attachment and aversion and so forth. All these are nothing but offshoots of grief (*soka*) — symptoms of the disease known as *samsara,* ocean of grief.

An enlightened being also lives in this world and functions through the medium of body and mind. Seeing them, ignorant people who mistake the body for the 'Self,' might think these great souls also have a sense of duality. However, they are totality detached from the body and fully centered in the Self.

Look at Lord Shiva's *damaru* (small drum he holds in one of his hands). The instrument looks like two triangles meeting one another at the apex. Both ends are wide and the middle is narrow. Hidden in this image is the highest spiritual secret. The individual self, jiva, and the Supreme Self, Shiva, are, in reality, united. They are one and the same. Individuality is nothing but totality in a specific name and form.

I first saw Amma one evening in 1979. I came with many questions. I thought of voicing some of them: would I fare well in my B.A. (Bachelor's Degree) exams, the future, and other similar queries. Those who accompanied me to Amma said, "You don't need to tell her anything. She will tell you everything." I decided to find out if that was true.

At the time, I didn't know even the ABC's of spirituality. I also didn't have any idea about the great guru that Amma is. The only information I had was from the incomplete and not so convincing explanation given to me by my companions. Furthermore, in that state of mind, I had given utmost importance to the matter of getting an answer to the question, 'Life, what next, to resolve the anxiety about the future?' Whether to become an actor, singer, or something else was the most important decision I wanted to make.

Half-way across the backwaters in a ferry, I could hear the undulations of a song. Though it came from the other side of the backwaters, the voice was soulful, and had an unearthly allure. As we got closer to the place, the singing became more audible. It was Amma singing. Her voice was certainly different. It had an indescribable and a very special dimension to it. Did it have the power to spontaneously open one's heart? Yes, I thought so...

The song Amma sang was,

*ammē bhagavati nitya kanyē dēvi*
*enne kaṭāksippān kumbiṭunnēn*

O Mother Divine, the Eternal Virgin, I
bow to Thee for Thy gracious glance

At that time, there was neither a Mata Amritanandamayi Math, nor an ashram. The only buildings
then were the house where Amma's parents stayed,
a tiny temple and an adjoining shed made from
thatched coconut leaves. Nonetheless, the environment had a mesmerizing appeal to it; there
was such a compelling attraction about the place!

As I stood in front of the temple, one of those
who had come with me whispered in my ear,
"Want to sing some bhajans?" I thought, "Why
throw away this opportunity?" I readily sang a
few devotional songs. As I sang in the small ve-
randa, my mind inadvertently became absorbed.
I thought Amma, who was giving darshan inside
the shrine to the devotees, looked at me once or
twice... No, she did, for sure!

Amma told me, "As you were singing, Amma
knew that this voice is meant to merge in God. At
that moment, Amma bound you with her mind."

"To bind me with her mind...!" I didn't understand what Amma meant by that. But when my perception about life took a hundred and eighty degree turn after my first meeting with Amma, the experience itself was a clarification of the statement Amma made.

On that first day, when my turn came, I went close to Amma to receive her darshan. When I reached her, the questions I had been entertaining in my mind until just a few moments before, slowly began to melt away like snow in the heat of the sun. The moment I was in Amma's arms, I was unable to say anything to her. In those eyes and in her face, I beheld an ocean of compassion.

The only way I can verbalize the experience is... 'It was like drinking in the love and affection of all the mothers in the world, an overwhelming experience of touching all that love right there, in that moment.' A huge tidal wave from that ocean engulfed me. What followed was indescribable. The experience was like a homecoming after long years of exile; like a prisoner who was in jail for many years being released in a moment he was least expecting it. It was a little like a sick old man returning to his teenage years. Maybe the experience was closer to a beggar being blessed with the magical lamp of Aladdin for no apparent reason. Even these examples are inadequate to compare to the bounty and wholeness of the experience.

Without my knowing, the doors of my heart flew open. Tears gushed forth, tears of bliss overflowing from my heart. Hugging me tightly, Amma whispered into my ears, "Child! What is it you seek? You are mine, my son, and I am your mother… " And then, Amma disclosed everything I had in my mind. But I was in a state where my mind and words had been erased. That was the moment I realized that everything I had considered 'important' in life was totally 'unimportant!'

Words fail me to adequately describe my first encounter with Amma. This description is just the 'tip of the iceberg,' an itsy-bitsy part of trying to present to you in a tangible form — what was my intangible experience.

That was forty years ago… how fast time has passed; how many changes have taken place! The ashram has matured into a huge organization with branches throughout the world, millions of devotees, humanitarian activities that cut across national boundaries, compliments and recognition from the United Nations and countries outside India for those activities, amazing revolutions Amma is achieving in the fields of education, medical science and research, and the international honors that come seeking her. The list goes on.

Amma is the symbol and representative of the ancient wisdom of the exalted lineage of the rishis, the seers of India. Hence, she is beyond all barriers of language, nationality, culture, color, etc. Her life is meant for the upliftment of the entire humanity. To put it in Amma's own words, "To me, the whole world is like a flower. Each petal represents a country. If one petal is infested by pests, the others will also be affected. I love the flower as a whole because the beauty of the flower is in its wholeness."

The *Maha Upanishad*, a part of *Samaveda*[5] tradition, says:

> *ayam bandhurayam nēti gaṇanā*
> *laghucētasām*
> *udāracaritānām tu vasudhaiva*
> *kuṭumbakam*

---

5 One of the four Vedas.

The distinction 'This person is mine, and this one is not' is made only by the narrow-minded (i.e. the ignorant who are in duality). For those of noble conduct (i.e. who know the Supreme Truth), the whole world is one family (one unit). (6.72)

Amma is the very embodiment of this Upanishadic statement.

But, in spite of everything, she remains the same as ever. Amma's life reminds us of Lord Krishna's words: '*kutasthamacalam dhruvam*'—'That which is unchanging, still and eternal.' (*Bhagavad Gita*,[6] 12.3)

To put it in Amma's own words, "There were times when people had strewn my path with thorns. In those times, and now as well, when people disperse flowers on my path, I remain as That. I have always been one with The One."

If the teacher were not in the class, what fracas, what noise, would prevail! But if the students so

---

6 'Song of the Lord.' It comprises the teachings Lord Krishna gave Arjuna at the beginning of the Mahabharata War. It is a practical guide for facing a crisis in our personal or social life and is the essence of Vedic wisdom.

much as saw the teacher's shadow looming from a distance, they would sit still and keep quiet. Similar is the effect that the presence of souls like Amma have. By their mere presence, *sannidhi matrena*, everything happens.

I have heard a poem where God was depicted as the ruler of the universe who manages everything by the mere movement of His eyebrows. How is that possible? Does God have an eyebrow? Even if He does, how can He control the universe by the mere movement of His eyebrows? Such doubts may arise. To be honest, I don't know much about this matter, for like everyone else, I don't have much knowledge about such a God. But I have seen everything working out in the right way, at the right time, just by Amma's mere presence.

One can learn everything just by watching Amma. Her life is a perfect reference book of life for people of all nations, languages, cultures and religious beliefs. In her life, we find the supreme example of true meditation, genuine love, compassion, selflessness, patience, forbearance and determination. Amma shows us how to interact with all kinds of people—even our enemies. Daily, she exemplifies how to deal with children of all ages, perfect management of the mind as well as external situations, time management, waste management, disaster management, even money management and all other aspects of life.

There is an art to Amma's every action. By this, I don't mean that she is an artist. Instead, she is art itself—Goddess Lakshmi and Saraswati[7] incarnate. Amma is not a singer, but her songs reach deep down to touch human hearts and create waves of love and bliss therein. Amma is not an orator, but her words manifest a transformation in people's hearts. Amma is not a dancer, but when she dances, we forget ourselves in bliss.

Every one of us has two births. The first is when we emerge from the mother's womb. The second takes place when we find a Satguru. Babies are innocent, but their innocence doesn't last for long. As they grow, their egos will grow, too. However, when we meet a Satguru, the innocence within us is reawakened. The inner child who was lying dormant is reborn. When we look at this universe with those eyes of innocence, everything will be a page in the book of virtues, a divine message

---

7 The goddesses of wealth and knowledge respectively.

from God. Gradually, we rediscover our innate state of innocence.

When I first came to see Amma in June 1979, I was reborn as a child. I was 22 years old. Since then, I have been holding onto the hem of Amma's sari. That continues to this day. Forty years have passed, but before Amma I am still a child. That's how I like it. If one is a child, one can learn a great deal. It's also easy for a mother to teach a child. The portals of knowledge become closed to us the moment we think, "I am grownup and have become big." Alternatively, it is easiest to grow if our heart becomes expansive and our ego shrinks.

Even though 40 years have passed, that transforming first experience of Amma's presence and the words she intoned in my ears back then still resound in my heart. Amma's presence is my Dwaraka. She is my Krishna. From her emanates the eternal song of love, the divine music of pure, unconditional love!

Amma's life and deeds are my object of meditation. Her voice and words are, for me, the sounds of the Divine Flute—the sweet melody that roused me from deep slumber.

# 5 | SAHASRAPADE NAMAH[8]

*rāmam daśaratham viddhi mām viddhi*
*janakātmajām*
*ayōdhyām aṭavīm viddhi gaccha tāta*
*yathāsukham* (Ayodhya Kanda, 2.40.9)

This verse has been acclaimed as the most important in the *Ramayana*. It appears in the following
context: Lord Rama and his holy consort Sita Devi
were ready to leave for their exile in the forest.
Accompanying them was Lakshmana. That is
when Sumitra advises Lakshmana, her son, "Son,
see Rama as Dasaratha, Sita (daughter of Janaka)
as myself (Sumitra), and the terrible forest as Ayodhya; have a safe journey and return."

This verse has an esoteric meaning too. *'Dasa'*
means 'ten.' Through this word, Sumitra was hinting that Sri Rama should be seen as one of the ten
incarnations of Lord Vishnu. The word *'maam,'*
therefore, can be interpreted to mean Goddess
Lakshmi (Lord Vishnu's consort). In other words,

---

8  "Salutations to the Goddess, who has a thousand feet."
(*Sri Lalita Sahasranama*, mantra 284)

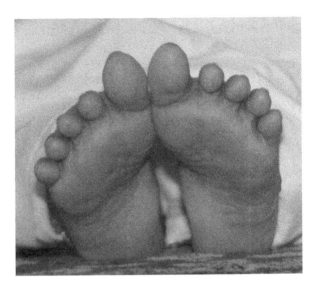

what Sumitra meant was, "Remember that Sita is none other than Goddess Lakshmi Herself."

What about the forest? It is that which none has been able to conquer, i.e. Vaikunta, the impregnable abode of peace, which enshrines Lord Vishnu. "O son, with this resolute faith, go forth happily and return safely." In short, the verse means, 'Where Lord Rama dwells, there indeed is Ayodhya, the true abode of peace, even if it is the forest. And where the Lord is not, that place becomes a forest.'

To put it briefly, where there is the divine presence of a Self-realized soul, that verily becomes Ayodhya. Ayodhya means the place without *yuddha* (conflict, war), the ground of supreme peace. Wherever in the world a Self-realized master is, that place becomes transformed into a sphere of everlasting happiness and beauty. The 'atmosphere' there transposes itself into '*Atma*-Sphere', a space where you can experience expansiveness of your inner Self.

An incident that happened a few years ago at the Gold Coast retreat in Australia comes to mind. We reached there after programs in Melbourne, Sydney and Brisbane. The enchanting venue for Amma's darshan and place of stay was near the sea, on a long shoreline of pure white sand. It is a popular holiday destination, with tens of thousands of people from all over the world coming to surf and relax.

The program lasted three days. On the third day, darshan continued until dawn. The return journey to India was that night. That evening, Amma came out of her room quite unexpectedly and walked straight to the beach. As soon as they saw her, devotees converged from various quarters, like bees honing in on nectar-laden flowers in bloom.

Being with a perfect master is such a profound experience. The attraction is irresistible. It is like iron filings and a huge powerful magnet. Nothing can stop the metal particles from getting attracted to the magnet. If someone tells them, "Stop flocking. Why don't you stay away?" it won't work. Just as it is the nature of the magnet to attract, it is the nature of metal to gravitate towards a magnet.

In pure love, the mind stops and thoughts cease to exist. Thinking doesn't have much of a place even in ordinary love. In fact, too much thinking ruins love. Thinking belongs to either the past or the future. Love is in the present. When two people fall in love, they don't think, "Should I, should I not." It just happens spontaneously.

I have heard, "Love cannot be explained or understood. When asked "Why do you love?" the answer is "I don't know. I just do." Because, love does not come from the mind to know, but from the heart to feel.

The *Brhadaranyaka Upanishad* says,

> *ēṣa prajāpatir yad hṛdayam, ētad brahma,*
> *ētad sarvam; tad ētat tryakṣaram; hṛdayam*

*iti. hṛ ityēkam akṣaram; abhiharantyasmai svāś cānyē ca, ya ēvam vēda; da ityēkam akṣaram, dadatyasmai svāś cānyē ca ya ēvam vēda; yam, ityēkam akṣaram; ēti svargam lokam ya ēvam vēda.*

This is Prajāpati — this heart (intellect). It is Brahman, it is everything. *'Hṛdayam'* (heart) has three syllables. *'Hṛ'* is one syllable. To him who knows as above, his own people and others bring (presents). *'Da'* is another syllable. To him who knows as above, his own people and others give (their powers). *'Yam'* is another syllable. He who knows as above goes to heaven (*svarga*)." (Not the heaven where you spend the rest of your life enjoying pleasures, but the state of eternal bliss, oneness with pure consciousness.) (5.3.1)

The 'heart' referred to in this verse is not the blood pumping organ as in physiology. This is the spiritual heart, the center of the human body, where we experience all the deep feelings. People all over the world say, "My heart opened up when I saw him or her." "My heart is closed." "My heart ached for those who lost everything in the disaster." Amma always says, "Open your heart and pray."

As translated, the Sanskrit root of the word 'hrdayam' is comprised of three syllables: 'Hr' means to draw, to attract. You become the center of attraction. You attract even the whole universe. 'Da' stands for 'giving' in both ways. You give everything to everyone, and they too give everything to you. This includes the entire creation. Now the third syllable, 'yam' means 'to go' to ascend to the highest peak of existence. This is the ultimate meaning of hrdayam, the heart.

The heart is the most impenetrable aspect of the body. The Upanishadic verse quoted above talks about this heart, the God within us, the innermost recesses of an individual.

The *Bhagavad Gita* says:

> *īśvaraḥ sarva-bhūtānām hṛddēśē'rjuna tiṣṭhati*
> *bhrāmayan sarva-bhūtāni yantrārūḍhāni māyayā*

The Lord, dwells in the hearts of all beings, O Arjuna, and by His Maya,

causes all beings to revolve, (as if)
mounted on a machine. (18.61)

This is why we meditate on the heart, because that is where God is seated, the point where you feel the 'you' in you. This is the reason why most people all over the world consider the 'heart' the most refined, natural and simple point of the body.

Now, returning to the story where we left it… Surrounded by the devotees at the beach, Amma stood with her gaze fixed on the horizon. Her mood and the expression on her face were beyond our comprehension. After some time, Amma cupped some seawater in her palms and reverentially raised the water to her forehead and offered the water back into the ocean. She then closed her eyes gently.

While Amma's face bore the majesty of profound peace, the devotees remained still, fixing their gaze on her, basking in that blissful presence. Slowly, Amma opened her eyes. She then started walking into the sea. Without waiting for permission, the devotees also followed her. "Children, be careful. Stand with your feet firmly embedded in the sand," advised Amma lovingly. When the water reached just below her knees, Amma stopped.

After a few minutes of meditative silence, she raised both her hands to the sky and sang, *"Srishtiyum niye, srashtavum niye, saktiyum niye, satyavum niye... devi... devi... devi..."* ("You are creation. Creator, too, You are. You are the Supreme Power and the Truth. O Goddess..."). The devotees sang, too, repeating each line with utter abandon. As the sound of the ocean waves continued to chant the sacred syllable "Om," the waves of thought in the minds of the devotees subsided.

Amma blissfully sang another bhajan, *"Kotanu koti varshangalai satyame tetunnu ninne manushyan..."* ("Man has been seeking You, O Truth, for aeons..."). When the song ended, the pure vibrations created by the bhajans invoked an inner stillness, despite the sound of the crashing waves.

"Let's go. It's already dusk!" When they heard Amma's voice, devotees regained their sense of place and time. A crowd of people had gathered and were watching: people strolling by, joggers, swimmers, surfers, and those who had come to enjoy some solitude. I overheard some say, "She's the Hugging Saint." Another person said, "I would like to experience the warmth of her embrace." Soon the Gold Coast seashore became yet another darshan venue, illumined by the hues of sundown. This was not something new. During Amma's travels, every setting is a darshan venue for her, including airports, airborne planes, roadsides, parks and government buildings all over the world.

When the seaside darshan ended, Amma started walking up the beach. Suddenly, an idea struck me. It was a natural yet powerful inner call. "Amma has stood all this time in the water. Aren't the sands sanctified by the touch of her holy feet?" Before Amma could move away, I bent down and grabbed a handful of sand from under her feet. She started walking ashore. I reverentially saluted the sand in my palms. I stood looking at Amma as she trudged ahead on the beach with the devotees.

The next moment, Amma turned around and said to me, "Son, how much love and devotion you have for the handful of sand taken from where Amma stood. But you've forgotten one thing, my son. Every grain of sand on this earth bears the imprint of Amma's feet. She has trod on each and every speck. Therefore, son, you should strive to develop the same love and reverence you have for that handful of sand towards all objects, big and small, in the world, towards every atom."

Those words were brimming with her customary love and motherly affection. But they went beyond the comprehension of my mind and entered the deepest recesses of my heart. I do not claim to have fully grasped the meaning of those revelations that were equal in depth to scriptural statements. Amma's words were profound and powerful. They were capable of quieting my mind for some time. I experienced a glimpse of the truth of Amma's statement, "Every grain of sand on this earth bears the imprint of Amma's feet. She has trod on each and every speck."

The *Purusha Sukta* (Rig Veda) says,

> *ōm sahasraśīrṣā puruṣaḥ sahasrākśah*
> *sahasrapāt*
> *sa bhūmim viśvatō*
> *vṛtvā'tyatiṣṭhaddaśāṅgulam*

Thousand-headed is the Purusha (the Cosmic Being), thousand-eyed and thousand-legged. Enveloping the earth

from all sides, He transcends it by ten
fingers' length. (10.90)

In this verse, the transcendental totality of the
entire creation (earth) is referred to as Purusha, the
Cosmic Being. The word 'dasangulam' represents
the ten fingers. It is believed that in the human
body, the distance of the heart from the navel
area is ten fingers. The figure 'ten' is symbolic
of 'infinity.' This is because it is considered that
numbers go only up to nine. Everything above is
deemed as numberless.

The heart is the seat or the home of Atma or God.
The navel symbolizes the origin of the manifested
world. That is the reason why we see a lotus flower
with a long, supple stalk emerging from the navel of
Lord Vishnu. We also see Lord Brahma, the creator,
seated in the lotus. The Cosmic Being's infinite nature is veiled by the glitter of worldly objects.

Looking at that extraordinary marvel of a being, Amma, who had just briefly uncovered the
treasure-trove containing the gems of universal
truth and was now laughing and playing with
the devotees in total innocence, as if ignorant of
everything, I was dumbstruck. I was still holding

on tightly to the handful of sand from under Amma's feet. Amma and the devotees were still walking. At that moment, she turned around to look at me. There was a mischievous grin on her face, "Son, why are you still standing there? Come quickly!" called Amma.

When I heard Amma's call, I did not tarry any longer. I ran towards her. We have a long way to go before we reach that expansive sky of consciousness that Amma embodies. So, let us hearken to Amma's call. We must walk with her and strive to keep pace with her.

"Every grain of sand on this earth bears the imprint of Amma's feet. She has trod on each and every speck." This lofty utterance still pulsates with my every heartbeat. I can still hear the reverberations from that mantra of power. It continues resounding in my ears, heart and every atom...

The one and only wish of Amma, the Satguru, is that all her children should also grow to become like her, as expansive as the sky, thereby attaining the state of Universal Motherhood. Hence, Amma constantly tells us, "Children, you are the divine essence of Om. Grow as endearing ones and merge in the eternal Om."

# 6 | GURU IS GOD EMBODIED

God is a transcendental Being. That indecipherable power is beyond human comprehension. The very inconceivable nature of God makes it most effortless for people, especially the so-called atheists and agnostics, to deny the existence of an absolute power that controls the universe. Conversely, there are eminent scientists who believe in the 'mystery' of the universe. Albert Einstein is one of the most revered scientists ever. He was quoted as saying, "Everyone who is seriously committed to the cultivation of science becomes convinced that in all the laws of the universe is manifest a spirit vastly superior to man, and to which we with our powers must feel humble."

Srinivasa Ramanujan, the mathematician who is considered to have been a genius, openly admitted that the Goddess (Namagiri Devi) revealed the most complex mathematical formulas to him. Similarly, Sir Isaac Newton remarked, "What we know is a drop; what we do not know is a vast ocean. The admirable arrangement and harmony of the universe could only have come from the

plan of an omniscient and omnipotent being." I can keep quoting many more…

A close devotee of Amma who works at the Los Alamos National Laboratory, USA, recently shared something with me. Once, Leon M. Lederman, a particle physicist who won the Nobel Prize for Physics in 1988, visited the Los Alamos lab. While he was talking to a group of high school students, one of the students asked him whether he had any message for the students. He replied, "I don't know, I don't know, I don't know." What he meant was that our attitude should be 'how little we know about anything in the universe.' Thus, he was emphasizing the importance of humility. He has written a book called *Symmetry and the Beautiful Universe*. Leon M. Lederman believes that everything in the universe is interconnected, from the tiniest of atoms to the magnificent cosmos. He was the one who coined the word 'God's Particle' for Higgs Boson.

Thousands of years before the emergence of modern science and much before contemporary scientists began to venture into the mysteries of the universe, the Hindu scriptures — the Vedas and the Vedantic scriptures in particular — with undisputable logical argumentation and analysis, established the existence of a super intelligence known as God, or the supreme consciousness, the one and only reality behind the diverse world. There must be a mysterious and timeless spirit that maintains the harmonious and orderly movement of this universe, which exists in ever-changing time. The ancient rishis called this 'Brahman,'

Absolute Consciousness, the Supreme Self, the one without beginning, middle or end. They described that Transcendental Being as "smaller than the smallest and bigger than the biggest," beyond words, mind and intellect. Here is a Sanskrit verse from the *Kathopanishad* for your reference:

> *aṇōraṇīyānmahatō mahīyānātmāsya*
> *jantornihitō guhāyām*
> *tamakratuḥ paśyati vītaśōkō dhātuḥ*
> *prasādānmahimānamātmanaḥ*

> Subtler than the subtle, bigger than the biggest, in the heart of each living being, the Atma reposes. One free from desire, with his mind and the senses composed, sees the glory of the Atma and becomes absolved from grief. (1.2.20)

The word 'Bharatam' (India) means that which is devoted to light, the brilliance of knowledge. Nowhere else can such ecological/biological diversity and magnitude be found. The ancient rishis, born in India, inquired into the mysteries of the universe and realized the oneness behind the diverse world. Ancient India had masters in every single branch of knowledge as evidenced by the following:

- Acharya Aryabhatt — Master Astronomer and Mathematician
- Bhaskaracharya — Genius in Algebra
- Acharya Kanad — Expert in Atomic Theory
- Rishi Nagarjuna — Wizard of Chemical Science
- Acharya Charak — Father of Medicine
- Sushrut — Father of Plastic Surgery
- Varahamihir — Eminent Astrologer and Astronomer
- Patanjali Maharshi — Proponent of the Science of Yoga
- Bhardwaj Maharshi — Pioneer of Aviation Technology
- Kapila Maharshi — Father of Cosmology and many more…

As Amma says, "The rishis never considered science and spirituality two. For them science and spirituality were complementary, not contradictory."

Even though the ancient seers described the ultimate reality of the universe as nameless, formless and changeless, that which is without a beginning, middle, or end, they also believed that this principle is the essence of everything in creation, both sentient and insentient. Hence, through a life of severe *tapas* (austerities), they proved to the world that every human being has the capacity to realize this inherent truth. The *Kathopanishad* says:

> *yadā sarvē pramucyantē kāmā yē'sya hṛdi*
> *śritāḥ*
> *atha martyō'mṛtō bhavatyatra brahma*
> *samaśnutē*

> When all desires clinging to the heart
> of one fall off, then the mortal becomes
> immortal and here (while alive) attains
> Brahman. (2.3.14)

But the Upanishad also clearly states that this supreme knowledge cannot be imparted by an inferior person who only has knowledge gathered from books.

> *na narēṇāvarēṇa prokta ēṣa suvijñēyo*
> *bahudhā cintyamānaḥ*
> *ananyaproktē gatiratra nāstyaṇīyān*
> *hyatarkyamaṇupramāṇāt*

When taught by a man of inferior understanding, this Atma cannot be truly known, even though frequently contemplated upon. There is no way (to know It) unless it is taught by another, an illumined master), for it is subtler than the subtle and beyond argument. (1.2.8)

The Upanishads are the words of Self-realized masters. These seers of the ultimate Truth are trying to express the inexpressible, that which is beyond the mind and words. So, the language they used to share their subjective experience is bound to be subtle in nature. It may sound like a contradictory puzzle to an unenlightened person who is not established in the supreme Brahman. Such people cannot impart this supreme knowledge about the Self, the very core of our existence. However, there is no question of any doubt, or variation, when this subtle knowledge is transmitted by a knower of the Self, someone beyond all sense of duality. This is the purport of the above verse.

Religious texts of all faiths depict God as the most compassionate being, the embodiment of all virtues, such as pure love, self-sacrifice, self-lessness, nobility, humility, simplicity, fearlessness and so forth.

Is it possible to speak with such a God? Can we see, touch, feel, and experience a God as portrayed in the scriptures? The search to find a God endowed with these qualities has existed since time immemorial. And the realization occurred to many, in the past and present, that the God they were searching for was within, not outside. It also dawned on them that the awareness of this pristine truth would transform one into a personification of all the divine qualities of God, as mentioned in the Hindu scriptures. Having unveiled the mystery of existence, these enlightened spiritual masters shared this precious knowledge with those who were in a quest to know the truth about God, thereby giving birth to the tradition of a guru-disciple relationship. It continues even today and shall continue in the future as well. In the presence of these extraordinary beings, one gets a glimpse of God. An open-minded and non-judgemental person, someone who is serious about verifying reality, can behold the glory of

God, the limitless love, compassion and other virtues of God.

We call a physicist by that name, because he or she has gained deep knowledge of physics, the interactions between matter and energy. A talented actor, singer or painter is known as a gifted artist. Likewise, we have virtuous and blessed doctors, teachers, leaders and so forth. Don't we recognize and value them? Yes, we do.

One extraordinary talented artist, scientist, or teacher can train and shape another extraordinary genius or disciple. We have so many such personalities who excelled in every area of action and then passed on the knowledge or talent. It is all about 'knowing the subtleties' of that art form or science. Without remaining on the surface, or periphery, they choose to dive deep into the knowledge of that subject. They gain a certain degree of identity, oneness with that knowledge. For example, unless an actor who enacts the role of a tribal man is capable of imbibing the mannerisms and life of a tribal person, at least to some extent, he will fail to present the character in a touching and impactful way. Here, the actor must have some degree of identification with the character he plays. Similarly, we have singers and musical instrumentalists, who can sing and play like celestial beings and keep their audience mesmerized for hours on end. This is possible because they are realizing the soul of the art form. It is not uncommon for people to address these exceptionally talented people as an incarnation of that subject or art form. In a similar manner, one who knows the totality, Brahman, becomes one with That absolute reality. Therefore, the *Mundaka Upanishad* says:

> *sa yō ha vai tat paramam brahma vēda*
> *brahmaiva bhavati nāsyābrahmavitkulē*
> *bhavati*
> *tarati śōkam tarati pāpmānam*
> *guhāgranthibhyō vimuktō'mṛtō bhavati*

He who knows that highest Brahman becomes Brahman indeed; and in his line, none who knows not the Brahman will be born. He crosses grief and virtue and vice and being freed from the knots of the heart, becomes immortal. (3.2.9)

A perfect spiritual master, who is permanently established in that state of oneness, the unalterable truth of existence, is actually God, the extraordinary in an ordinary human form. Observing them, we will come to understand that God exists. Through them we can behold God's glory, feel God's power and experience God's beauty. Such a spiritual being serves as a bridge, a link between God and the world, an impeccable communicator between the world of names and forms and the nameless and formless Supreme Being. Only he or she is capable of leading others along the path to God.

Amma gives a striking example. "A stranger visits a house where a woman and her seven-year-old child were home alone. The husband had gone to run some errands. The lady feels a little awkward to present herself in front of a stranger. Now, what is the easiest and most effective way to manage this situation? She can stay in her room and send her son to the man to find out the purpose of his visit. The boy can freely move back and forth between his mother's room and the living room where the stranger is sitting to communicate their messages, correct? In a similar manner, the guru has the freedom to move between the empirical world of happenings and the unknown realm of God. The Satguru is the bridge that connects us with the supreme. He or she is familiar with both worlds."

For a disciple, there is no other God than his or her guru.

The *Svetasvatara Upanishad* categorically states,

> *yasya dēvē parābhaktiḥ yathā dēvē tathā*
> *gurau*
> *tasyaite kathitā hyarthāḥ prakāśante*
> *mahātmanaḥ*

> These truths, when taught, shine forth only in that high-souled one who has supreme devotion to God and an equal degree of devotion to the Guru. (6.23)

Infinite is the power of a true spiritual master who is ever established in the ultimate state of Self-realization. The real question is, how can we identify such a guru? On the battlefield of Kurukshetra, Arjuna, posed the same question to Lord Krishna.

> *sthita-prajñasya kā bhāṣā samādhi-sthasya*
> *keśava*
> *sthita-dhīḥ kim prabhāṣēta kim āsīta*
> *vrajēta kim*

Lord, what is the disposition of one
who is always established in the state of
supreme consciousness? How does an
enlightened person talk? How does he sit?
How does he walk? (2.54)

Through the next eighteen verses, Sri Krishna elucidates eighteen clear signs to recognize a sthitaprajna, one who abides in the exalted state of pure awareness.

This list details the signs of a perfect soul, as described by Lord Krishna in the *Bhagavad Gita*.

1.  The sthitaprajnas are beyond all conflicts of the pairs of opposites (*dvandatita*). They are totally free from all likes and dislikes, attachments and aversions. They have no sense of 'I' and 'mine.' They accept all dual experiences of life, such as pain and pleasure, virtue and vice, honor and dishonor, and good and evil equally.

2.  The sthitaprajnas' life is a perfect example of the ultimate reality of the Atma, the Self, the potential divinity of all beings. Through word and deed, the sthitaprajnas express the unity and oneness of all existence.

3. Regardless of the changing external circumstances, the sthitaprajnas will ever be established in the unbroken state of bliss, the nature of the inner Self. Nothing affects a sthitaprajna's pure knowledge or jnana.

4. Sthitaprajnas are the extraordinary in ordinary human form. Since they are also living in this world, they may behave like ordinary human beings, yet they are constantly aware of the absolute reality, the supreme oneness.

5. Being utterly egoless, sthitaprajnas have no doer-ship attitude, no claims. They may perform actions, but those actions don't bind them, as they are not identified with their body and mind.

6. Sthitaprajnas are always calm and composed, peaceful and happy. Even in the midst of total chaos, they remain unperturbed.

7. Sthitaprajnas' knowledge is born out of their awareness about the oneness of the totality, the existence. Their wisdom transcends all forms of worship, places of worship, spiritual practices and scriptures.

8. As sthitaprajnas are one with the universal consciousness, their freedom is infinite. There-

fore, they don't have to adhere to the customs and habits of a society, traditions, scriptural dictums, etiquettes and so forth. They may still follow them, but the practices will not bind them in any way. At the same time, the sthitaprajnas will neither force their freedom on anyone, nor will they disrupt the rules and regulations, or code of conduct, set by society.

9. Sthitaprajnas belong to everyone. They belong to the world, to all nations, to all cultures, to the entire creation. They exist for the benefit of all beings, of all times. Their very nature is love and compassion. The sthitaprajnas consider the whole universe their abode.

10. Sthitaprajnas have no expectations whatsoever. They are the rulers of the universe because they have no desires and are perfectly in control.

11. Sthitaprajnas are not blessed, but blessing itself. They are purity embodied and the personification of supreme knowledge. They are permanently established in the highest spiritual experience, sahaja samadhi, from where there is no return.

12. Sthitaprajnas may not necessarily be people of words but deeds. They are a perfect role model for all people from all walks of life.

13. The sthitaprajnas' existence in the world is just on the borderline of the empirical world of happenings and supreme consciousness.

14. In sthitaprajnas, one can see a confluence of all the spiritual paths. They are perfect *bhaktas* (devotees), *karma yogis* (one who follows the path of selflessness) and *jnanis*, epitomes of Advaita Vedanta (non-dual philosophy). Depending on the circumstances and need, they can be anything they wish.

15. Fully established in the state of perfected equal vision and non-attachment, sthitaprajnas have no friend or foe. Ever content in their own Self, they see those who insult them and glorify them equally.

16. Having realized the absolute Brahman, the one with no beginning, middle and end, the never born and deathless Self, sthitaprajnas are totally fearless.

17. For sthitaprajnas, God is with form and without form, limited and limitless, immanent and transcendent.

18. Sthitaprajnas give equal importance to all spiritual paths. As everything is pervaded by God consciousness, nothing is insignificant or unimportant. For them, there is no matter, nothing is insentient, because God alone exists, consciousness alone is.

Verse 18 in the 5th chapter of the *Bhagavad Gita* says:

> *vidyā-vinaya-sampannē brāhmaṇē gavi hastini*
> *śuni caiva śva-pāke ca paṇḍitāḥ sama-darśinaḥ*

> The knowers of the Self look with an equal eye on a Brahmin endowed with learning and humility, a cow, an elephant, a dog, and a pariah.

Let me share an incident from Amma's life to illustrate the depths of this verse. I, myself, was witness to this incomparable act of compassion on the very first day that I met Amma. Dattan, a leper, used to come for darshan regularly. It was so touching and at the same time awe-inspiring to see how Amma showered her love and compassion on him, even though his body was totally disfigured and covered with pus and blood-oozing wounds. Because Amma regards everyone as her child, she would embrace him with the same love and compassion as she showed everyone else, perhaps even more. While hundreds of devotees were watching, Amma used to lick his festering wounds with her tongue. For those who witnessed what was taking place, it was both horrifying and deeply moving. In due course, Dattan was completely cured. His only medicine was Amma's saliva. All his wounds disappeared and only the scars remained on his body.

Avatars or the incarnations of God such as Amma are like the wind. They blow everywhere—on the mountains, through the valleys, in the Ganges as well as in muddy and stagnant waters, on both posh buildings and slums, on both fragrant and itchy flowers, and upon both virtuous people and those with vices. There is absolutely no feeling of worthiness or unworthiness.

A Satguru is also known as an avatar of God. In fact, a true Satguru verily is an avatar. There is no doubt in my mind that Amma is a unique incarnation of God. I believe that all those devotees who truly observe Amma's life and her actions share the same belief.

Is there a difference between a Self-realized soul and an avatar, you may ask?

From the level of the highest spiritual experience, there is no difference. Essentially, they both are eternally absorbed in the state of sat-chit-ananda. But objectively speaking, there is a difference. The fundamental difference between an avatar and an enlightened being is that the former will have infinite compassion, love, selflessness, patience, forgiveness and self-sacrifice. Their whole life will be dedicated to the upliftment of society. They lead other spiritual aspirants who are in the pursuit of God to the goal. To put all these in one sentence, 'an avatar is the embodiment of compassion.'

Conversely, an enlightened soul, even though established in the same exalted state of oneness, remains immersed in supreme bliss, totally unconcerned about the world and those who are lost in it. Back in the early 80's Amma gave us many opportunities to be in the presence of such enlightened beings. Though their oneness with the supreme was so obvious and tangible, they were totally disconnected from the everyday happenings of the world. They didn't care about anything or anyone; they were not at all conscious of their bodily existence, their surroundings, nor the pain and sufferings of others. That gave us a beautiful contrast between the state of an avatar and an enlightened being. Their consciousness level and realization are the same, but the way they chose to be in this world seemed to be completely different.

In reality, an enlightened soul, alone, has the inner power to choose. As they are one with the infinite, their choices are also infinite. They have no barriers.

Back in the early 70's, soon after Amma began to manifest Devi Bhava, her father Sugunanandan, thinking that his daughter was possessed by some divine being, demanded that Devi should leave his daughter's body. Naturally, he was concerned about her physical and mental well-being. He also wanted her to lead a normal life. So, he went inside the temple during Devi Bhava and insisted 'Devi' relinquish Her hold on his daughter's body. Amma responded saying, "If I give you back your daughter, she will be nothing but a corpse and will soon start decomposing, and you will have to bury her!" Nevertheless, Sugunanandan was adamant. He vehemently continued his request. Finally, Amma said, "In that case, here is your daughter. Take her!" Instantly, Amma fell down on the spot. Her body became stiff, her heart stopped beating, and there was no breathing. She was dead from every appearance.

Full of remorse and shedding profuse tears, Sugunanandan implored the Divine Mother to bring his daughter back to life. The devotees who came for Bhava Darshan were stricken with grief and prayed fervently along with Sugunanandan. Eight hours passed before there was a slight movement in her body and she returned to life.

This incident shows how a Self-realized soul can die consciously and re-enter the body consciously. While we all die unconsciously, once we learn how to die, we can choose our birth and death. It is perfectly under our control. The body is the object, while the Atma, the Self, is the Subject, the pure consciousness.

Amma says, "We often hear people saying, 'the pain of death.' Nowhere in the world do we hear someone saying, 'the bliss of death.' In fact, if the ego is totally eliminated, just as we celebrate our birthday, we also can celebrate our death. When we die consciously, we know that death is only the death of the body. Once the ego dies, we experience unconditional freedom."

The body (the object) is a conglomeration of the five elements of space, air, fire, water and earth. It has its own limitations and is bound to change, decay and return to its original source. On the other hand, the subject, the Atma, the Self, the pure energy we are constituted of, is different. It is the same as everything we hear, touch, see, taste and smell, everything sentient and insentient, everything gross and subtle, all facts and also the mystery. Once we realize this inherent oneness, we are, indeed, one with the universe. We are the universe. It is like a seed becoming a tree. In reality, the seed is a tree in a dormant state. This awareness transforms and reveals the unbounded potential within us, the immeasurable energy we truly are. This uncovering of our true nature opens the door to infinity.

We human beings claim to enjoy a great deal of freedom. Nonetheless, the reality is that we are bound by countless limitations. The free will and freedom of choice we think that we have exists only in our dreams. In most circumstances, we act like a cow with a rope tied around its neck and the other end tied to a tree. So, if you ask, "Do we have freewill?" Yes, we do, but with only as much as a bound cow has.

A disciple once asked the guru, "Master, how much freedom of choice do I have?"

The master instructed the disciple to lift one of his legs. The disciple raised his left leg.

"Now raise your right leg also," said the master.

"How can I? I will lose my balance and fall down, right?" replied the disciple.

The master smiled and explained, "Right you are. So, your freedom of choice ends with raising one of your legs. Before lifting your leg, you do have the freedom to raise either the right or left leg. However, once you are done with the act of raising one of your legs, there your freedom ends."

We can find references to animal sacrifice in the Vedas and other ancient Hindu scriptures. The Sanskrit word used to cite this is 'pashu.' Even though the most common meaning of this word is 'cow,' it also means cattle or animal in general. The etymological origin of the word seems to be the Sanskrit root, 'pash,' meaning rope, symbolic of bondage. So, the real meaning of the usage pashu is a reminder that we all are captives of the ego, that we are all bound by ignorance. The reins of our life are in the hands of the ego, our lack of true knowledge and awareness. It indicates that, instead of living a life established in our true being, we live a totally self-centered life, bound by the ropes of our lower emotions. So, when the rishis said to sacrifice 'pashu,' what they actually meant was to go beyond the animalistic tendencies, transcend them, renounce the ego and be free.

There is a constant fight going on in our lives between our past, 'what we were,' and the future, 'what we want to become.' This is how the ego is formed. In between the past and future is the 'present moment,' the dwelling place of real peace and happiness. Unfortunately, we keep missing this moment and are being unceasingly pulled by the future, the desire for *karma phala* (the result of our actions). This experience is enormously intense and persistent. We feel like the cow with a rope tied around its neck, incessantly pulling the person holding the other end of the rope. When this fight stops, or when this is renounced, we become totally free.

What is it that makes us limited, finite and bound? Our wrong notions about life, the world, our relationship with people, objects and our own physical existence. This fundamental misconception generates a fetter of unintelligent attachment to everyone and everything we come into contact with. Amma says, "When we label life as, 'my life,' 'your life,' 'his or her life,' etc., we are, in fact, creating a division, which in reality doesn't exist. All demarcations are only in your mind and thoughts. They are just concepts of the mind. In reality, life is the totality of consciousness."

Life is most priceless for all of us. This is an indisputable truth. Nevertheless, what do we know of life? Do we know anything about its greater dimension, its infinitude nature? When we say, 'my life,' do we ever think that we are only referring to a 'piece of sky' we see through the peephole of our mind? Of course, that tiny 'piece' is part of the endless sky. That piece we behold, verily, is one with the sky. Realizing that and living in that awareness of the totality is what a Satguru helps us to discover.

A perfect master is one who has transcended all misconceptions created by the limited ego, the body, the mind including emotions, the world, and objects of the world. His awareness level has reached its peak. He is one with the infinite sky, the totality of existence. Hence, he has the inner capacity to choose because the freedom he enjoys is seamless and unadulterated.

The ultimate union with God is so absorbing that one may tend to forget the world and one's own physical existence in that incomparable bliss. An enlightened being can remain totally oblivious to the world and unconcerned about the suffering of people. They may not help, guide and take responsibility for people groping in darkness or those in search of God. They can also be immensely compassionate and, thus, be in the world, with the people, guiding and uplifting them. Such a phenomenon is known as an avatar, a Satguru.

Let me share a few incidents with you, which I am sure will help you understand what I mean:

Ottoor Unni Namboothirippad was an eminent scholar, poet and ardent devotee of Lord Krishna. He became a permanent resident of Amma's ashram in 1983. He was eighty five years old at that time. He was like a little child in front of Amma. Amma lovingly called him, 'Unni

Kannan' or Ottoor-*mon* (son). Ottoor's one and only wish, his only prayer to Amma, was, "Amma, when I breathe my last, let my head rest on Your lap. This is my only wish, my only prayer. O my Mother, please let me die with my head on Your lap." This prayer was repeated fervently to Mother whenever he met her.

Just before Mother's third World Tour in 1989, Ottoor's health took a very bad turn. His condition became extremely serious, and he was completely bedridden. Everybody, including the doctors, thought he was going to die. His only fear was that he would die when Mother was abroad.

One day Ottoor expressed to Amma his fear of dying before Amma returned from her US tour and thereby not fulfilling his earnest desire to be able to die in Amma's lap. Amma caressed him affectionately and replied with great authority, "No, my son, that will not happen! Be sure that you will leave your body only after Amma's return." This was a great consolation to Ottoor as this assurance came directly from Amma's own lips. Ottoor firmly believed that death couldn't touch him before Amma came back.

This is exactly how it happened on the morning of Friday, August 25th, as Mother had predicted earlier: Ottoor breathed his last with his head resting on Amma's lap. The point is that, when Ottoor feared that he would die before Amma came back from her trip abroad, Amma so emphatically told him, "No, my son, that will not happen! Have no doubt that you will leave your body only after Amma's return." The question is, who else but a Satguru such as Amma, who has conquered death and gone beyond the sense of birth and death, can command death not to touch her devotee without her permission?

Yet another, most amazing part of Ottoor's life is that he had written a song twenty five years before Amma took birth on earth. The relevant parts of the poem are as follows:

> *kaṇṇande puṇya nāma varṇaṅgaḷ*
> *karṇattilennu kēḷkkum ñān...*

When will I hear the auspicious names of Krishna in my ears....

The last stanza of the song goes like this:

> *āṭṭavum kazhiññammatan maṭi*

*taṭṭilēkennu vīzhum ñān*
*vīṇumammatan śītalānkattil*
*sānandam ennurangum ñān*

When will I finally fall into my Mother's lap after the play has been enacted? On falling on my Mother's lap, when will I sleep blissfully?

As the great devotee of the Lord wished, he left his body while resting his head in Amma's lap, beholding his beloved Krishna's beautiful form on her countenance.

It shows how an incarnation of God, such as Amma, fulfills the sincere and wholehearted prayers of a true devotee.

There is an incident in the life of the great woman saint, Mira Bai, who is still remembered for her unconditional love and surrender to Lord Krishna. One of the kings of Mewar (in modern day Rajasthan) became very jealous of Mira's popularity and decided to poison her. She gladly accepted the cup of poison and drank it after offering it to Krishna first as was her habit. A wonderful thing happened. The poison Mira Bai drank became harmless nectar. She was unaffected, but the idol began to change its color due to the poison's effect.

There was a dog, who was very close to Amma. He was like a faithful servant and guard to her. In the early 80's, the dog got rabies and was chained to a tree. Even though all of us tried to prevent her, Amma went up to the dog and fed it with her own hands, caressed and kissed it. We wanted Amma to take injections against rabies, but Amma said, "No problem. Nothing will happen."

These incidents point out the oneness of these great masters with the universe, with God, with infinity.

For people like us, love means just personal relationships. However, 'Love' as a universal principle is impersonal. It is beyond all barriers of religion, nationality, language, humanity, animals, plants, etc. It transcends everything, all names and forms. It becomes formless. In that state, nothing affects you, because you de-identify with your body totally.

When Amma initially began to receive people by embracing everyone who came to see her, there was a great deal of protest and disapproval from the villagers and her own family members. From one angle, the disapproval of the family was understandable because a young girl hugging people of all ages, regardless of gender, was not at all part of the culture. One of their major concerns was that nobody from a reputable family would come forward with a marriage proposal for the girls in the family.

When all their efforts failed to stop Amma from continuing her "strange behavior," one of her cousins locked her in a room and brandished a knife threatening to take her life if she did not stop her way of embracing people. Amma was unperturbed and did not yield even an inch to the cousin's request. She calmly told him, "Kill me if you wish. You can only destroy the body. The soul is imperishable. Come what may, I'm not going to change my ways under any circumstance. This, indeed, is my dharma. I want to offer my life to the world, to comfort and console the suffering people until I breathe my last. I completely surrender myself to this cause." Imagine the world today if Amma had become afraid and had given in to their threats! Just a few words, "Yes, I will obey you," would have changed history. Having witnessed Amma's power of will, her fearlessness and the firmness in her words, the cousin was bowled over and left the room utterly exasperated.

Only a true spiritual master such as Amma, who is one with the universe, who is fully aware of the mysteries of life, who is totally fearless, who is established in pure unconditional love, can help us in this process.

Amma, out of sheer compassion, chose to be in this world to lead people from "Untruth to Truth, Darkness to Light and from Death to Immortality." As declared in the scriptures, such a great master, a Satguru who has known Brahman, the ultimate reality is verily Brahman itself. They are God embodied.

# 7 | A HEART AS EXPANSIVE AS THE SKY

The world is familiar with only one type of love, better known as 'attachment.' This emotion, though generally interpreted as love, is not real love, because attachment can move in the opposite direction and become aversion at any time. In other words, attachment, which is attraction to a person or object, is like a mask. Hiding beneath the mask is aversion, or repulsion.

Today you love someone because he or she pleases you. If the same person criticizes you tomorrow, your love turns to hate. Basically, either you like a person or an object, or you dislike them. So, all our emotions fall under two categories: 'like and dislike.' When you like someone, you are attracted or attached to that person and, at other times, dislike overpowers you.

Our wrong perception makes us believe that love is not possible, without two entities. In fact, love is both with form and formless. The 'two' can merge into 'one' and eventually transcend all dualities. In the *Bhakti Sutras* of Narada, the sage says,

> *sā tvasmin parama prēma rūpa*
>
> Bhakti, is the absolute love towards the Supreme Being. (2)

Such bhakti, or pure love, is not an emotion. It is undying in nature, whereas emotions come and go, fluctuating and volatile.

We cannot love someone, or something, without a reason. 'I love him because he is handsome.' 'She is my boss, so I like her.' Emotions are temporary. When a close friend or relative dies, you feel sorrowful for some time. Then you forget them. People going through a divorce experience mental agony for some time, then they move on to another relationship.

The *Bhagavad Gita* says:

> *mātrā-sparśās tu kauntēya śītoṣṇa-sukha-duḥkha-dāḥ*
> *āgamāpāyino'nityās tans-titikṣasva bhārata*

> Notions of heat and cold, of pain and pleasure, are born, O son of Kunti, only of the contact of the senses with their objects. They have a beginning and an end. They are impermanent in their nature. Bear them patiently, O descendant of Bharata. (2.14)

Real devotion, love for love's own sake, goes beyond the mundane world of likes and dislikes. It is losing oneself, one's ego, into the vast infinitude of God. The following poem authored by Mira Bai, the unparalleled devotee of Lord Krishna, will give us a glimpse into the highest form of love:

> Unbreakable, O Lord,
> Is the love

That binds me to You:
Like a diamond,

It breaks the hammer that strikes it.
My heart goes into You
As the polish goes into the gold.
As the lotus lives in its water,

I live in You.
Like the bird
That gazes all night
At the passing moon,
I have lost myself dwelling in You.

I am reminded of Amma's words, "All over the world, people say, 'I love you.' It sounds as though 'love' is trapped between 'I' and 'you.' We should embark on a journey from 'I love you' to 'I am love,' because that is the truth of our existence. We are the formless love, the embodiment of love."

Amma says, "When you are established in love, the state of love is rather impersonal. In that state, your attitude is not, "I love this person" or "I love that person." Watch Amma to get a deeper understanding of this concept. She simply loves.

She is love. Amma is always available. As Amma says, "Like a river, I just flow."

For a great master such as Amma, permanently established in the state of pure awareness, the bliss of existence is her very nature, and the sky of consciousness is her innate abode. Relationships such as mother and children, guru and disciple, friend and foe do not exist in that state of awareness. The only experience is *Shivoham*: I am Shiva, the unconditional consciousness. These celebrated lines from Sri Adi Shankaracharya's *Nirvaanashatkam*, a distillation of the Supreme experience, come to mind:

> *na bandhūr na mitram gururnaiva śiṣyaḥ*
> *cidānanda rūpaḥ śivō'ham śivō'ham*

> I have neither kin nor comrade, neither guru nor disciple.
> I am pure awareness and bliss. I am Shiva! I am Shiva! (5)

The mind and body, attachment and liberation, action and inaction all exist only on the empirical level. Beyond all these is indivisible consciousness without a beginning, middle or end.

What existed before creation, i.e. before what modern science dubs the 'Big Bang?' Even scientists have only theories about it.

The Hindu scriptures proclaim that the universe emerged from the sacred syllable OM. The diversity of life emerged from a single principle. In other words, the universe manifested from nothingness. Though formless, that 'nothingness' wasn't an absence or emptiness, but the presence of a super intelligence, the subtlest and most powerful form of energy, the essence of everything, the whole universe.

The *Bhagavad Gita* says:

> *paras tasmāt tu bhāvō'nyō'vyaktō'vyaktāt sanātanaḥ*
> *yaḥ sa sarveṣu bhūtēṣu naśyatsu na vinaśyati*

> But distinct from that Unmanifested is the other eternal unmanifest Reality, who does not get destroyed when all beings get destroyed. (8.20)

> *avyaktō'kṣara ityuktas tam āhuḥ paramām gatim*

*yam prāpya na nivartantē tad dhāma*
*paramam mama*

He who has been mentioned as the
Unmanifested, the Immutable, they
call Him the supreme Goal. That is the
supreme abode of Mine, reaching which
they do not return. (8.21)

There is a beautiful story in the *Chandogya Upa-nishad*:

Shvetaketu, the inquisitive son, asked his fa-ther, Uddalaka, a great sage, "Why am I not able
to see the Atma if it is all pervasive?"

"Bring me a fruit from the *nyagrodha* (banyan)
tree outside," said his father. When the boy re-turned with the fruit, the father told him to break
it and look inside.

Asked the father, "What do you see?"

"I see some seeds, father, exceedingly small,"
replied the son.

"Break one of those."

"It is broken, father."

"What do you see there?"

"Nothing…"

In response, the father said, "My son, can this marvel of a tree come out of nothing? It is simply that you are unable to perceive the subtle essence of the tree contained inside the seed. In that very essence stands the being of the huge banyan tree. Know that essence carries the substratum of the whole of existence. That is the Truth, that is the Self, and thou, Shvetaketu, art That."

The *Taittireeyopanishad* says:

> *so, akāmayata, bahusyām prajāyēyēti,*
> *sa tapō, atapyata, sa tapastaptvā, idam*
> *sarvamasṛjata, yadidam kiñca, tat sṛṣtvā,*
> *tadēvānuprāviśat, tadanupraviśya, sacca*
> *tyaccābhavat, niruktam cāniruktam ca,*
> *nilayanam cānilayanam ca, vijnānam*
> *cāvijnānam ca, satyam cānṛtam*
> *ca satyamabhavat, yadidam kiñca,*
> *tatsatyamityācakṣatē.*

He (the Supreme Self) desired: "May I be many, may I be born. He performed austerities. Having performed austerities, He created all this—whatever there is. Having created all this, He entered into it. Having entered into it, He became both

the manifested and the unmanifested,
both the defined and undefined, both
the supported and unsupported, both the
intelligent and the non-intelligent, both
the real and the unreal. The Satya (the
True) became all this: whatever there is.
Therefore (the wise) call It (Brahman) the
True. (Brahmananda Valli 6:6)

Perhaps this is another effective way of describing
the state before the 'Big Bang' and how creation
occurred.

Amma's words sparkle with ancient glimmers
of the supreme truth. They contain universal
truths in hidden, seminal form. That is why
the utterances of spiritually illumined souls are
considered sacred law. That, indeed, is the reason
why these universal truths are known as *Sabda
Pramana* (authoritative verbal testimony of the
absolute Truth). In order to understand them, the
mind must become meditative.

A Satguru's teaching doesn't necessarily have
to be verbal. The guru's methods are mysterious.
The disciple should have the love and patience to
observe the guru constantly. Innocent love for

the guru can establish a smooth and unperturbed connection with the guru. In that love, the guru's silence and every movement can be decoded.

Don't we seek the guidance of a native speaker when we want to learn a new language? Similarly, the ultra-subtle language of spirituality is unknown to us, whereas for Amma, it is her real abode, her mother tongue, her very own method of communicating.

In a student teacher relationship, teaching involves a classroom, a certain time, an atmosphere, prescribed textbooks, and so forth. Conversely, in the guru-disciple relationship, teaching happens all the time, in all circumstances. Whether they appear significant or insignificant, the guru's actions, words, silence, anger, smile, glance, the twitching of her eyebrows, the movements of her eyes, everything is capable of revealing one more layer of the unknown.

Spiritual knowledge is the subtlest of all knowledge. The medium of communication cannot always be verbal. In fact, words are very limited and, hence, may distort the truth. Therefore, observing the guru is most important. If the disciple has the determination, sincerity and love, his or her observation will gradually evolve into meditation.

To be a student is easy, but to be a disciple requires tremendous courage and love. While the former is only an intellectual exercise of accumulating information, the latter is forgetting all that you have gathered from the world outside and making yourself fully available to the guru for her to re-create you. Hence, Amma says, "In a true guru-disciple relationship, it will be difficult to distinguish between the guru and the disciple. This is because the guru will be humbler than the disciple." Amma adds, "The patience of the guru is the refuge of the disciple."

A disciple is like a fledgling, just hatched out of the egg. It can't fly like its mother. Looking at its little wings, the fledgling wonders if it would be able to perform the same 'feat' as the mother bird. The baby bird also wishes to soar high and own the sky, but it is scared to do so. Watching its mother doing the 'impossible,' the baby bird gradually develops an intense yearning to fly. It flaps its little wings but is unsuccessful even to rise from its nest. At one point, the mother takes over and encourages her little one to gather the courage to fly. She even demonstrates her flying skills in front of the baby bird, as if inviting, persuading and attracting the fledging to follow her example, as though telling her baby, "Don't worry, my dear, I am here to protect you and prevent you from falling." Then, there comes a time, when the mother seems to be a little ruthless, ruthlessly compassionate to be precise. She pushes the baby bird out of the nest into the open air. Lo and behold, the baby bird spontaneously opens up its wings and flies out of the nest. That push is needed or else the little bird will remain inside the cocoon of fear and lose its inherent potential. The mother bird in this anecdote represents the Satguru.

A Satguru such as Amma is also like a true mother. For disciples to establish an absolute relationship with the guru, they must have the attitude of a child. While in the womb, every baby is fully one with the mother. The baby eats, sleeps, breathes through the mother. It is a bond so deep, it is undetachable. The disciple should have a similar bond with the guru, but with greater depth and intensity. Such an innocent relationship is the finest path to unlearn and relearn, to undo and redo everything in the Satguru's presence.

As far as the disciple is concerned, they are completely unaware of the intricacies of the spiritual journey they embark on. Both the journey and the destination are totally unknown to them. While visiting a new city or country, we take the assistance of an expert guide who is thoroughly familiar with every nook and corner of the place, right? The key to spiritual realization is just one word — trust.

Let me tell you a story. A little girl dropped her doll, and it broke. Seeing the broken pieces of the doll, she started wailing loudly. With tears in her eyes, she told her brother, "I'll pray to God to join the broken pieces of this doll together."

"Will God listen to your prayer?" The brother asked, expressing his doubt. He then delivered his verdict, "I don't think so!"

"God will definitely answer my prayers," declared the girl with utmost faith.

After a long time, the brother asked his younger sister, "Did you receive any answer?"

With absolute belief and trust, the girl said, "Yes. God said, 'It can't be repaired!'"

A child's sole refuge is its mother. If we can learn to become a child in our hearts, we can earn a place in the heart of Amma who is as expansive as the sky. She will hold us close to her bosom and take us across the ocean of samsara, of endless grief.

Amma says, "The guru's love has a universal presence. Therefore, the physical boundaries of time and space cannot restrict its flow."

In 1999, my cervical disc prolapsed. It was a time of intense pain and suffering. Amma was the first to warn me about what might happen. We were on Amma's annual North India tour. Just after the last program in Bangalore, Amma gently touched my shoulder while sitting behind me in the car. The moment Amma touched me I somehow knew that the touch was special. It was full of concern, love and other profound feelings. When Amma touches us, looks at us, it is always special, but each time when Amma touches us, looks at us, it tells us something different; there is a different message. Her hands spoke, her eyes spoke, Amma's whole body spoke to me.

As we were on tour, I was treated at a hospital in Mumbai. After visiting me in the hospital, Amma left for her Mauritius and Reunion tours. I was bed ridden for almost three months. It was a very trying time. Ultimately, the doctors prohibited me from playing the harmonium ever again. They said the excessive strain on my neck could cause a recurrence.

In those days playing the harmonium while singing bhajans for Amma had become such a joyous part of my life. Singing and playing the harmonium were, in my mind, inseparable. It was heart-breaking for me to think of no longer playing the harmonium. Because Amma was already in Reunion, I could not seek her guidance on the matter.

After I left the hospital, I was staying with a close devotee family in Mumbai as I had travel restrictions due to my neck condition. I was feeling immensely sad thinking about not ever being able to play the harmonium again. I had no other choice but to cry and pray to Amma for her grace and guidance.

There was a special room in that house where Amma used to stay whenever she visited Mumbai. The family had converted it into a meditation room. I went there, and sitting next to Amma's bed, I cried and prayed with my whole heart to Amma. In about half an hour, the head of the family came to the room. He handed over a cordless phone and said, "Amma is on the line from Reunion Island."

I told Amma about the doctor's advice. After listening, Amma calmly replied, "Don't worry, my son; you will be able to play the harmonium and sing again."

I asked, "When?"

Amma said, "Today..."

"Today...!" I was overjoyed.

"Today, when, what time?" I asked.

Amma said, "In the evening, when Amma begins the evening bhajans, just as Amma sings the first bhajan, the Ganesha song, you play the harmonium and sing. But only one bhajan for the time being."

And this is exactly what happened... When Amma began the evening bhajans in Reunion Island, I was sitting in the very same room where Amma had stayed in Mumbai, gratefully playing the harmonium and singing:

> *śrīpādamāhātmyam ārkkariyām... guru*
> *pādattin vaibhavam ārkkariyām*
> *śrīpādamāhātmyam ārkkariyām... guru*
> *pādattin vaibhavam ārkkariyām*

Who knows the greatness of the lotus feet of the guru? Who knows the grandeur of the guru's feet?

# 8 | BIRTHDAY GIFT

There are those who argue that the guidance of a guru is not necessary in attaining the ultimate realization of the Self. This may be true in the case of a seeker endowed with tremendous samskara, spiritual wealth accumulated and inherited from previous life times. Even such rare souls may need someone to push them into the final state of total emancipation.

Amma says, "There is a stage in a seeker's life when he or she has done everything possible. Having made all efforts, there comes a standstill point, where the aspirant has nothing else to do but wait for the final realization to dawn. Standing at a threshold, he knows not what to do next. He has been waiting and waiting. When nothing happens, there is a likelihood of the seeker becoming exasperated. Losing patience, he may turn away from the goal and fall back into the world thinking, 'There is no such thing known as Self-realization.' At that point, all that the sadhak needs is a push from someone, a perfect master who has travelled the path and arrived at the final destination."

Relying on the scriptures alone can easily confuse the seeker. The rishis must have had great difficulty communicating their experience of the infinite using finite words. In their efforts to reveal the deepest mysteries of the universe, the sages must have carefully chosen minimal words in communicating their experience to the world. Each word is a seed, capable of growing into a huge tree of knowledge. Every word is pregnant with the truth behind creation.

Studying the scriptures is like entering into a dense forest. It is so enchanting, but at the same time, it is deceptive as well. Why so? Because, the truth is buried deep inside the wrapper of poetic language. The sages were creative and learned people, hence their writings contained literary flourish.

Though the supreme truth is one, the scriptures describe and interpret it differently. There are thousands of commentaries. Without the help of a Satguru, it is extremely difficult to understand and imbibe the hidden meanings, varied implications, apparent contradictions, illogicalities and intricacies of the scriptural aphorisms.

In the *Bhagavad Gita*, Lord Krishna says,

*tat viddhi praṇipātēna paripraśnēna sēvayā*
*upadekṣyanti tē jñānam jñāninas tattva*
*darśinaḥ*

Know that, by prostrating thyself, by
questions, and by service; the wise, those
who have realized the Truth, will instruct
thee in that knowledge. (4.34)

A Satguru is more feminine than masculine.
A perfect master has to be motherly in nature
because only a mother has the virtues of understanding, patience and love that are indispensable for the child's growth. While an ordinary
mother's heart can only expand to contain her
own children, a Satguru's heart is as expansive as
the universe. Being in the presence of a Satguru,
serving her and allowing her to discipline you, can
be compared to being in a mother's womb. Allow
the guru to give to you, your real Self. By doing
so, you gain the whole universe. But before that,
you have to lose many things.

Once a man asked a spiritual aspirant, "What
did you gain by surrendering to God?"

He replied, "Nothing... but let me tell you
what I lost: anger, ego, greed, depression, insecu-

rity and fear of death. Sometimes, the answer to our prayers is not in gaining, but in losing, which ultimately is the gain."

Buddha said, "I can only say I have lost something—the ego, the mind. I have not achieved anything at all. Now I know that all that I have was always there. It was in every layer, it was in every stone, in every flower, but now I recognize it was always so. I was blind then, but I have lost my blindness; I have not achieved anything, I have lost something."

Reporters ask Amma, "Are you an avatar, an incarnation of God?"

Amma spontaneously responds to this question saying, "You are also an avatar. Everyone is divine. Everything is pervaded with God. That is what we are."

*Moksha* (liberation and total freedom from the body, mind, and intellect) is not an individual experience, although it seems like that from our perspective. For him or her, the dawning of that supreme realization is also the disappearance of all imperfections, which, in actuality, are only external. This means that the whole world attains perfection. The ultimate spiritual realization is normally described as the subjective experience of a particular individual. Nevertheless, for him or her, the awakening happens to the entire creation. This is because, from that moment onwards they see everything pervaded with pure consciousness. Once established in that state of consciousness, the sun rises, never to set again. A Satguru can bestow this knowledge on the disciple, provided the disciple has innocent faith in the guru.

There is a beautiful story of Thotakacharya, one of the main disciples of Adi Shankaracharya, the exponent of Advaita Vedanta.

Sri Shankara had four main disciples, Padmapada, Hasthamalaka, Sureswara and Thotaka. Of all four, Thotaka was considered to be unintellectual and dull. However, his true devotion for his guru was unquestionable, and he was always engaged in *guru seva* (selfless service to the guru) in some way or the other. One day, Adi Shankara was about to begin the scriptural class, but Thotaka was absent. He was washing the guru's clothes, one of his main jobs. As he was waiting for Thotaka to come, Padmapada, Sri Shanka-

1 Hymn of eight verses in praise of the guru.

ra's scholarly student, commented, "Anyway, he doesn't understand any of the subtle principles of the verses. So why wait?" To which Sri Shankara replied, "You have no idea about his tremendous faith in the guru."

Sri Shankara wanted to remove the false pride of Padmapada and demonstrate how guru-bhakti can bestow pure wisdom to the disciple, even without being adept in the scriptures. It is said that Sri Shankara glanced in the direction where Thotaka was engrossed in washing clothes and showered his grace on him. Thotaka was illumined. Knowledge dawned on him. That very moment, he strongly felt his guru's call, and he walked into the classroom reciting the famous, *Thotakaashtakam*,[1] which begins as follows:

> *viditākhilaśāstrasudhājaladhē*
> *mahitōpaniṣat kathitārthanidhē*
> *hṛdayē kalayē vimalam caraṇam*
> *bhava śankara dēśika mē śaraṇam*

O Thou, the knower of all the milk-ocean of Scriptures! The expounder of the topics of the great Upanisadic treasure-trove! On Thy faultless feet I meditate in my heart,

Be Thou my refuge O Master, Shankara!
(1)

Allow me to share an incident that took place on October 10th, 2006. The place was Crystal Palace in Central London, and the time, about noon.

A few days before this incident, my laptop crashed and had stopped working, so that morning I went shopping for a new computer with Dr. Vagees, a devotee from London. We went to a huge shopping mall that stretched for as far as the eye could see. You could get literally anything there. The search for the computer began. Meanwhile, my eyes were looking for something else too — a gift for Amma.

As it turned out, October 10th, 2006, was the holy day of *Kartika*, Amma's birth star. (September 27th is her birthday according to the Gregorian calendar.) I wanted to offer something to Amma on that auspicious day.

My eyes, which were wandering here and there in search of a suitable gift, suddenly fell on a cluster of necklaces. One in particular stood out. It was actually a choker, orange-coloured, and made of strands of intertwined bead necklaces. "If only

I could get it," my mind whispered. But what if it was too expensive? Amma totally disapproves of imposing on devotees by making them pay for any purchase. My attention turned away from computers and became riveted on the choker. I moved toward the glass display enclosing it and discreetly checked its price—£10 (about ₹800, US$20). Seeing this, Dr. Vagees asked, "What is it, Swamiji? What are you looking at?"

I didn't hesitate. I disclosed to the good doctor my heartfelt desire. When he learned that it was for Amma, his joy knew no bounds. We bought the choker; we did not buy a computer. Never mind, I thought. We needed to reach Crystal Palace before darshan ended. We got there by about 1:30 p.m. I went straight to Amma. When I took out the choker, Amma looked at me and asked, "What's this?"

"Today is Kartika, Amma's birthday." Saying so, I clasped the choker around Amma's neck, and prostrated. When I got up, Amma lovingly gave me a candy.

Amma spontaneously remarked, "I have no 'birthday.'" Her comment wasn't just a few casual words; however, only Amma could understand the true significance and inner essence of the words she just uttered. She genuinely meant what she said.

Looking at the choker, Amma asked, "How many strands are there?" She counted them and said, "There are 10." During darshan, Amma removed the choker and separated each of its strands. She put one around her own neck, and another around mine. "One for Amma, and one for my son," said Amma with a sweet smile. My heart was filled with contentment.

While standing near Amma, I casually told her, "I will be 50 next April 23rd. It will be my *'Amritavarsham50'* (name of Amma's 50th birthday celebrations)." When she heard this, Amma turned to look at me. In those eyes, I beheld a vast ocean of love and compassion. Gazing intently at my face, Amma asked, "Son, which desire would you like Amma to fulfil?"

I was stunned! I could not utter even a word. It was as if the supreme guru, prepared to bestow anything, was asking, 'Son, what would you like? I offer you anything and everything.' My mind became silent in amazement.

Ask for *bhakti* (devotion to the Lord), *mukti* (spiritual liberation) or *bhukti* (material prosperity). Amma will give it. This was the import of Amma's words and gaze. In those moments, I could palpably perceive the immense grace overflowing from that motherly heart. Amma's words were so meaningful, and they held such power and authority.

Dr. Geetha Kumar, who was helping to manage the flow of devotees coming for darshan, suggested, "Swamiji, ask for moksha!" Her words woke me from my reverie. Speaking slowly, I said, "If I attain moksha, Amma and I would become one. Then I may not be able to remain as a child before Amma, travel with Amma, sing with her, or lie in her lap. So for now, I don't want moksha. Instead, whenever Amma assumes a human body and comes down to earth, I want to be Amma's child, servant, worshipful devotee, disciple, a shadow ever following Amma; it would be enough if Amma fulfils this desire for now."

As I stood gratified at having been able to offer this sincere prayer at Amma's holy feet, the counsel of Sri Krishna, Lord of the *Bhagavad Gita*, arose in my mind.

*āścaryavatpaśyati kaścidēna-*
*māścaryavadvadati tathaiva cānyaḥ*
*āścaryavaccainamanyaḥ śṛṇōti*
*śrutvāpyēnam vēda na caiva kaścit*

Some see the soul as amazing, some
describe it as amazing, and some hear of
the soul as amazing, while others, even
on hearing, cannot understand it at all.
(2.29)

Allow me to address some doubts that might arise
in the readers mind. It is natural if you think, "A
gift for Amma? Why? Did Amma ask for it? No.
Absolutely not." Amma never asks for anything.
Being the Empress of the universe, why should
she? She owns the entire universe.

Swami Rama Tirtha is one of India's greatest
saints. He was born in 1873 and left his body in
1906, at the young age of thirty three. Swami
Rama used to address himself as *'Baadusha Rama'*
meaning, Emperor Ram, though he hardly had
anything of his own. He travelled to America
and stayed in San Francisco for a year and a half.
There, too, he used to call himself, 'Emperor
Rama.' People used to ask him, "You are not a

king. You don't own a kingdom. Yet you call your-self 'Emperor…!" His response would be, "That is why I am the Emperor. I am nothing, hence I am everything. I have no desires; therefore, I am the Emperor. An emperor who is full of desires is just a beggar with unfulfilled desires. I am ever content. That is what makes one an emperor—the whole universe belongs to me."

The following are his words:

> I am determined to thunder out in your
> bosom my Godhead, your Godhead,
> and proclaim it through every deed
> and movement. I am Emperor Rama,
> whose throne is your own hearts. When
> I preached in the Vedas, when I taught
> at Kurukshetra, Jerusalem and Mecca,
> I was misunderstood. I raise my voice
> again. My voice is your voice, "Thou Art
> That." Thou art all thou seest. No power
> can prevent it; no kings, devils, or gods
> can withstand it. Inevitable is Truth's
> order. My head is your head, cut it if you
> please, but a thousand others will grow in
> its place. Beating in thy breast, seeing in
> thy eyes, throbbing in thy pulse, smiling

in the flowers, laughing in the lightning, roaring in the rivers, and silent in the mountains is Rama.

In the 10th chapter of the *Bhagavad Gita*, Sri Krishna tells Arjuna:

> *yad yad vibhūtimat sattvam śrīmad ūrjitam eva vā*
> *tat tad evāvagaccha tvam mama tejōm'śa-sambhavam*

Whatsoever being is glorious, good, prosperous or powerful, understand thou that to go forth from a fragment of My Splendor. (41)

Throughout the tenth chapter of the *Gita*, Sri Krishna lists many magnificent things in creation as manifestations of his glory: humans, sages, celestial beings, the most powerful, most beautiful, alluring, everything worldly as well as heavenly, celebrities in all walks of life. This means that they are all part of the infinite.

When Self-realized beings talk in the first person, they don't mean 'I' as a person, identified with the limited body and mind, but as the cosmic power, the limitless consciousness, which is not limited by space and time. In that sense, once you are one with your inner being, you are one with the universe.

That is the reason why the *Sri Lalita Sahasranama* describes Devi as *'Sri Mata, Sri Maharajni, Srimat-simhasaneswari…'* the Mother of the Universe, the Empress of the Universe.

Everything that one can see belongs to the vast empire of a Satguru, who is one with the totality. Offering anything, even the most expensive thing to a Self-realized master is like gifting Bill Gates with a laptop. However, there's another side to the issue. The disciple's life and all his actions are an offering to the guru. An ordinary mind cannot imagine the guru-disciple relationship, which may strike some as being irrational and idiosyncratic in so many ways. It is, indeed, no ordinary bond. It is the pinnacle of love. Here, the guru literally becomes everything for the disciple — mother, father, kin, guru and God, and a disciple's attitude is that of a child.

At times, the disciple with a heart filled with devotion, love and faith, may worship the guru. At that particular time, with tears in his eyes, he sings the praises of his guru and dances with abandon. At other times, he will humbly serve the guru, as a trusted confidant would his boss. There are also occasions when the disciple will bare his heart to the guru, as one would to a cherished friend. Instances also occur when the disciple will, like a child, prattle and throw tantrums before the guru.

Heed the utterance of Hanuman, the famed devotee of Lord Rama:

> *dehabuddhyā tu dāso'smi jīvabuddhyā tvadamśakaḥ*
> *ātmabuddhyā tvamevāham iti me niścitā matiḥ*

> O Lord, when I am identified with the body, I am Your servant. When I am identified with the jiva, I am a part of You. When I am identified with the whole Self, I am in truth nothing but You. This is my firm faith.

The Truth behind the diverse world is one, or oneness. In other words, diversity is wholeness in its manifested form. When one realizes this Truth, there is nothing that is not pervaded by Consciousness. *'Ekam sat vipra bahudha vadanti'*

(Truth is one; the wise know it by various names); *'sarvamidam aham ca brahmaiva'* (Everything, including me, is nothing but Brahman. In that highest level of consciousness, all divisions and differences disappear. One merges with the totality of existence. The experience of *Aham Brahmasmi* ('I am Brahman') dawns.

Amma, in her infinite wisdom, is guiding me every step of the way. I have no doubt that a time will come when I totally merge with the wholeness. That realization is the cessation of all likes and dislikes. Let it be. Still, I wholeheartedly pray, "O Amma, even after that, may I always remain as your child. May you forever be my mother."

Throughout my spiritual journey, Amma has always been holding my hand so tightly. As Amma says, "It is safer if the mother holds on to the child's hand. If it is the other way around, the child may run away unclasping the hold." I still feel like a toddler on the path.

We are forever at the mercy of the universe. We think our dreams and choices are the best for us. But our thinking may not be correct. Who knows what is in store for us, what the mighty universe holds for us? For our life to be fruitful, we need the full support and benevolence of all of existence. Nevertheless, it will only shower its blessing on us when we move in tune with its unalterable law, or dharma. Since we are incapable of conceiving anything without a specific name and form, we can pray, meditate and surrender to the Satguru, who is one with the totality, for grace and guidance. In the presence of a Satguru, the repository of infinite powers and compassion, the unfoldment of our Self will attain a new dimension, a beauty and charm beyond words. It will be so natural and spontaneous.

I would like to remind you of a lovely story and poem:

A young monk was walking with an older, more seasoned monk in the garden one day. Feeling a bit insecure about what God had in store for him to do, he was inquiring of the older monk. The older monk walked up to a rose bush and handed the young monk a rosebud and told him to open it without tearing off any petals. The young monk looked in disbelief at the older preacher and was trying to figure out what a rosebud could possibly have to do with his question.

Because of his high respect for the older monk, he proceeded to try to unfold the rose, while keeping every petal intact. It wasn't long before he realized how impossible it was to do so. Noticing the younger monk's inability to unfold the rosebud while keeping it intact, the older monk began to recite the following poem:

### Unfolding the Rosebud

It is only a tiny rosebud,
A flower of God's design;
But I cannot unfold the petals
With these clumsy hands of mine.

The secret of unfolding flowers
Is not known to such as I.
God opens this flower so sweetly,
When in my hands they fade and die.

If I cannot unfold a rosebud,
This flower of God's design,
Then how can I think I have wisdom
To unfold this life of mine?

So, I'll trust in Him, for leading

Each moment of every day.
I will look to God for His/Her guidance
Each step of this grace-filled way.

The pathway that lies before me,
Only God truly knows.
I'll trust Him/Her to unfold the
moments,
Just as God unfolds the rose.

Amma is helping all of us to unfold the mysteries
of life as we progress under her divine guidance.
We must leave that to her. Come what may, I
would always like to remain a child before Amma
and spend my life at her holy feet in her divine
presence as her servant. Therefore, even though
Amma, the Mother of the Universe, may not need
anything, this child, this servant who yearns to
do her bidding, wanted to give her a birthday gift,
even if it looked simple and frivolous.

# 9 | A CATALYST BEYOND COMPARE

There are skeptics and cynics. A skeptic provided with solid evidence may finally believe. The possibility of accepting the truth exists, whereas a cynic almost always has an unalterable mindset. The famous and quick-witted Groucho Marx, the American comedian, jokingly commented, "Whatever it is, I am against it." Most cynics move through the world that way.

I am reminded of the eminent astrophysicist, cosmologist and astronomer Carl Sagan's words, "One of the saddest lessons of history is this: If

we've been bamboozled long enough, we tend to reject any evidence of the bamboozle. We're no longer interested in finding out the truth. The bamboozle has captured us. It is simply too painful to acknowledge—even to ourselves..."

Skepticism can be classified as positive skepticism and negative skepticism. It would be highly beneficial both for society and individuals if skepticism and positivity (openness) were to go hand in hand. I have heard this saying, "Large skepticism leads to large understanding. Small skepticism leads to small understanding. No skepticism leads to no understanding." In essence, skepticism is valuable if skeptics accept and acknowledge truth when reality stares at them.

Normally, spirituality is considered a subjective science. This is true about many modern scientific inventions as well. Scientists find it difficult to explain some of the subtle principles of the universe. Hence, they come up with mathematical equations, because words fail to express the concepts.

I would say that Amma makes spirituality both subjective and objective. Skeptics and cynics, for their own reasons and beliefs, may deny the highest spiritual experience wherein great masters of

Amma's caliber are established. Just forget about the subjective spiritual experience which may be debatable, but can any sensible person deny the way Amma receives each and everyone who comes to see her, sitting hours on end. And this phenomenon happens seven days a week, 365 days a year, irrespective of place and time. I have to add that this is done with unquestionable affection, cheerfulness, without a word of complaint whatsoever, patiently listening to people's sorrows, showering them equally with love and compassion. This has been Amma's life for the last forty five years. So, when people skeptically ask, "What is so great about Amma?" I can only say, "Please come and watch her giving darshan." If you are in search of reality, which is the purpose of genuine skepticism, you may find the answer to your question.

Amma has a unique ability, an infinite inner capacity, to attract, inspire and bring out the best in people. For her, not just a handful, but every single human being is a seed that can grow into a tree, a promise to the world who can contribute to society. She views the world and the people in it free from the coloring of a selfish ego. Hence, Amma is forever empowering people, both materially and spiritually. Under her leadership, people learn self-management and the management of external circumstances, as well.

I have had the good fortune to travel with Amma around the world for more than thirty two years. I have personally witnessed the enormous change that takes place in thousands of people's attitude as they become inspired by Amma's words and actions. It is heartwarming to see little children, so used to thinking only of themselves, come to Amma with their piggy banks and tell her that they want to help children with no money. But it's not only about monetary or physical contribution to the charitable institutions. Thousands have given up negative habits. The small actions or gestures of kindness Amma inspires in people have so much power of transformation and affect the lives of so many people.

I'd like to share an incident that was narrated by Bri. Priya, who is serving as a gastroenterologist at Amma's hospital (AIMS), Kochi. A couple of years ago, one of her patients, an alcoholic, had developed bile duct cancer. He lived four hours south of the hospital and had come to AIMS with jaundice and severe itching all over his body. As he was an alcoholic and most of his family had abandoned him, he lived alone, working as a fisherman. Priya says that a common attitude people have towards such patients is, "Well… it's too bad for them. They were alcoholics for so many years. They had been told that alcohol will kill the liver. Now they have to suffer the results of their own actions." Though you might want to feel compassion towards these people, your mind drags you back to the thought, "They did it to themselves."

Once he was diagnosed with advanced cancer, he reacted in anger. He shouted at the nurses, doctors and basically anyone who came near him. He was one of those 'impossible' patients. Since there was no cure for his cancer, they offered him a temporary palliative procedure just to take away his jaundice and itching. The procedure was expensive and as a fisherman, he could not afford it, so the hospital had it done for free. The patient felt better after the procedure and left the hospital after a few days. Dr. Priya asked him to come back after a month so they could check if the temporary fix was still working. But, after one month, he never showed up.

Priya says, "I happened to notice that the patient hadn't come for his review. I mentioned this to my professor, but he said, 'He is probably drunk at home. He will come if he has a problem. Don't worry about him. He will shout at you if you contact him anyway.'"

Even though Priya thought the professor was right, Amma's words flashed through her mind, "Don't judge a person's behavior. They may have suffered in ways you cannot understand. Compassion should never have conditions." So, Priya decided to call the patient anyway. She called the number registered in his hospital file. Someone picked up and said, "Hello?" When she asked for the patient, the person on the other end said, "We have no delivery service here." Priya said, "I was confused. I asked for the patient again and the man got annoyed and said, 'No Soman works here.'" When she asked him where she had called, he said, "Mallan's Chayakkada." It was a roadside teashop near this patient's home.

Eventually Priya got a hold of the patient and asked him how he was doing. There was a long pause before he finally answered in a shaky voice, "Did you really call for me? No one has ever called me in my entire life. How did you even remember me?" He was so shocked. She could hear him sobbing over the phone. He could not get over the fact that someone cared.

A few days later, after the whole incident was over, Priya was on rounds in the hospital when she got a frantic call from the Gastroenterology outpatient department, "Dr. Priya! Please come fast! There is someone here with fish for you!" She thought someone was playing a prank on her so she just hung up the phone. After 10 minutes, they called back, "Please come right now. This man with fish is creating a ruckus in the department." Priya ran down more curious than anything else. When she got there, her patient was standing in chappals in the middle of the department, with a bucket of live fish swimming in water. She was so confused. She described what happened, "He ran up to me, put the bucket in my hands and said, 'I still cannot believe you cared enough to call me! I had to give you something in return. The best thing I could get are these fresh fish. I caught them myself. See! I even brought them in water so that you would have the freshest fish possible. Please take them.'" Priya said, "The man's eyes filled with tears as he watched me hold the bucket. He didn't even have money for proper slippers but he travelled four hours, stopping in between to change the water, just to give me a gift! I don't even eat fish but I took them anyway."

Just think of how our actions affect others... Such a seemingly insignificant act of making a phone call made a difference in this man's life. He died two months later, but the tea shop owner called Priya just to say that the fisherman kept telling everyone about his special phone call till the day he died.

This is just a single example, but knowingly or unknowingly, the small acts of compassion, humility, patience, courage and perseverance that Amma inspires in millions of people then percolate down to millions more. This is the indescribable transforming power of a true master such as Amma.

Some think that the ancient science of spirituality is life-negating, but instead, it is life-affirming. The ancient saints and sages valued and welcomed both external and internal wealth equally. This is the path that Amma follows, creating a beautiful blend of Science and Spirituality,

Matter and Spirit. For Amma, the world and God are not two, but one. Amma says, "Just as the sun doesn't need the light of a candle, God doesn't need anything from us. God is the giver of light. Around us, so many people are suffering. Let us console them. Let us give them the aid they need. This is true love for God. This is real spirituality."

Not far from our ashram in Chicago, Illinois, USA, there is a school serving a needy community. The families of the 900 children who attend this school are at or below the poverty line. Most of the children have no bus service, so they must walk to school, even though winter temperatures can drop to 29 degrees below zero. When the school approached our ashram for help, Amma responded in a novel way.

Here in India, women of Uttarakhand are still recovering from the 2013 floods. Many of them became widowed during the flood, and the knitting they have been taught by Amma's volunteers as part of the Mata Amritanandamayi Math disaster relief program is their only source of income. Before they began training in this craft, suicide and depression was prevalent amongst the flood survivors. Now, through Amma's guidance, over 60 women are engaged in knitting wool caps to keep the needy children in Chicago warm. In this story, there are no losers, only winners. The children of Chicago acquired warm clothing and a connection to a much broader world than they might have imagined existed. The women of Uttarakhand won financial remuneration, pride in their work, and the satisfaction of knowing their efforts were making a difference for others in need. But perhaps the true winners were the volunteers — those inspired by Amma to spend some of their time selflessly, thus benefiting the others in this story as they, themselves, became transformed and their minds and hearts were broadened by the special joy of serving under Amma's guidance.

Immediately after the catastrophic January 2010 magnitude 7 earthquake in Haiti, a team of Amma's devotees from the US led by Br. Dayamrita, was sent to Haiti to assess the situation as to what was needed and determine how Embracing the World could help. Arriving the day after the earthquake by private carrier, the only way of flying to the island because commercial carriers were barred from landing in Haiti, the team joined one of the hospital teams from Florida that had flown there to do surgery. Because the Haitians were disoriented and in a great deal of pain, many also not knowing what had happened to their loved ones, some of the most powerful time was spent comforting people, despite the language barrier. Without words, the team hugged people, sat with them, cried with them.

Of course, other things were accomplished as well. Despite total chaos in the country, somehow a source of rice and beans was found which was packaged and distributed to people who had had nothing to eat.

Hundreds of thousands of people died during the quake. For those who survived, life was overwhelmingly challenging. When it was evident that most of the homes near the highly populated epicenter of the quake were reduced to rubble, people were forced to live in the parks in the center of Port-au-Prince, the capital. Needless to say, with the rains slated to start soon, there would be no protection from the elements. Embracing the World was able to negotiate the delivery of a boatload of tarps from a company in Florida, which made a huge difference for thousands of homeless families.

During a subsequent visit to Haiti just weeks after the earthquake, it was evident that school children (many of whom were now orphans) were not able to afford tuition for school. Thirty children were identified who had lost one or both parents in the earthquake, and Amma offered to pay their school tuition monthly through high school, regardless of their age or grade in school, in an effort to keep them in school. Many of those students are graduating from high school now and are gratefully looking forward to careers as physicians and teachers.

The following paragraph will shed some light on Amma's vision of education, "The situation in education today is such that we need to specify a school as being one that provides a 'values-based education.' This implies that values are not an integral part of education, itself. But, the term 'values-based education' should, in fact, be considered redundant, because true education promotes an educational philosophy based on spiritual, moral, social and cultural development, enabling students to develop their own moral and ethical compass indicating what is right and what is wrong. Unfortunately, values and education have been dichotomized today. The factor stringing together life, individual, society and nature is missing from today's educational system. That missing element is spirituality — spiritual values."

Life's beauty and the experience of happiness are not dependent on increasing the quantity of things. The qualities you embrace are more important. Whether you are the head of a family, chief of an organization, or leader of a country, if you have a caring attitude, humbleness in approach, and the inclination to sacrifice your own personal interests and comforts for the sake of others, then you will be remembered, adored, and loved as someone who truly has no replacement. Your name and your actions will always remain as a guiding light to humanity.

Amma's spirituality is not disengaged from the world — it is verily embracing the world. For Amma, spirituality is not separate from life. It is very much part and parcel of our everyday life. For her, life is both logical and mysterious, perhaps more mysterious than logical. Amma creates a beautiful blend of these two aspects of life. As a perfect catalyst beyond compare, Amma transforms each life she touches.

# 10 | THE COMPELLING POWER OF SELFLESSNESS

"Atheism is impossible," according to studies conducted recently. Research scientists say that even atheists who proclaim, "There is no God!" believe in a majestic power without beginning or end. However, self-proclaimed atheists artfully conceal their faith.

Some scientists contend, "By birth, human beings are believers, not atheists. Faith in God is an intrinsic part of a person's genetic constitution and nature. It cannot be eliminated. Therefore, atheism is psychologically impossible."

In ancient times, as well as in this day and age, the majority of scientists believe in some paramount power. Those who set out to prove that there is no such power, perhaps consider themselves more knowledgeable and experienced than even those who have proven its existence through their direct experience. Given man's limited intellect, capable of ranging only within the confines of space and time, how can he prove the absence of a power that transcends such limitations?

Scientists attempt to confine the universe within space-time boundaries, circumscribing it within their 'scientific' laws. At the same time, we should remember the wormhole theory, as explained by the eminent scientist, Albert Einstein. The wormhole theory postulates that a theoretical passage through space-time could create shortcuts for long journeys across the universe. According to this theory, space-time bends under the influence of fields (e.g. a gravitational field). So, in order to travel from one point in space and time to another point quickly, one only has to bend space-time! The scientific world has not completely ruled out the possibility of this theory.

I have an interesting story to share. This took place in 1987, when we were on the initial trip through the United States, preparing for Amma's first visit there. It was two weeks into the trip, and I was missing Amma terribly. We were in Mt. Shasta in California at that time. My heart longed to hear Amma's voice. Back then, it was very difficult to place an international call to a remote village in India. In those days, the ashram had only one landline. I tried to place a call through a US operator to Paryakadavu/Vallikkavu, Quilon District, Kerala, as the phone I was using had no direct dialing facility. The operator had no idea where Vallikkavu or Quilon were. However, he agreed to give it a try. I waited in anticipation until past midnight. Finally, I went to bed with a heavy heart when there was no sign of getting connected.

I don't know what time it was, nor do I know if I was awake, asleep, or dreaming... suddenly the tepee (round, conical tent) wherein we were staying, became filled with a pleasant and soothing bright light. I could smell an unearthly fragrance. As I watched in awe, Amma smilingly walked into the tepee. She came close to my bed and most affectionately told me, "My son, don't be sad; Amma is with you." She repeated this message two more times and then was gone. She completely vanished.

And then, almost immediately, the phone rang. Did I wake up hearing the ringing sound, or was I already awake? I am not sure. When I picked up the phone receiver, it was the operator speaking. He said, "Connecting your international call to Quilon." In a few moments, I heard Amma's voice on the other end. She said, "My son, don't be sad; Amma is with you." She repeated this refrain two more times just as in the vision. And then, before I could say anything, the line was cut.

What was my inner feeling at that time? It is difficult to describe. It was intense. A quiet and still state of mind, but tears of an unknown joy rolled down my cheeks. That bliss didn't leave me for the rest of the night and for weeks thereafter...

The experience can be interpreted as an imagination of the mind, the fulfillment of a desire that was stored in my subconscious, maybe just a dream. Or one can argue that what I experienced was 'merely electrical brain impulses that pull random thoughts and imagery from our memories' which do not mean anything in particular.

Or, one can also explain it as the play of protons, neutrons and electrons. Whatever it was, a dream is a dream, without any real substance. However, my experience wasn't like that. It was very powerful, tangible to my senses. Therefore, rather than analyzing the experience from a scientific and logical point of view, I prefer to believe in Amma's divine power to 'bend space-time.' That faith gives me tremendous inspiration. After all, for someone who is capable of controlling the elements, it is not an impossible feat. This is what Einstein's 'wormhole' theory proclaimed to the world, right?

Albert Einstein also described the limited perspective of how we view time and space, "A human being is a part of the whole, called by us as 'Universe,' a part limited in time and space. He experiences himself, his thoughts and feelings as something separated from the rest—a kind of optical delusion of his consciousness. The striving to free one's self from this delusion is the one issue of true religions. Not to nourish the delusion, but to try to overcome it is the way to reach the attainable measure of peace of mind."

Whether Einstein was a believer or an atheist is debatable, but he always regarded the inherent order and recondite nature of the universe with wonder and reverence.

In my forty years with Amma, there have been an endless string of wondrous experiences, many inexpressible. Let me share one.

One day, a few years ago, while I was talking to some devotees in Amritapuri, a man joined the group. I hadn't seen him before. He seemed to be listening to the conversation. In the middle of the conversation, he suddenly posed this question to me: "What's so great about your guru, Amma?"

He didn't sound like a devotee, nor was his tone friendly. With folded magazines and a diary clutched under his arm, the man's facial expression and attitude seemed more like an interrogator.

When I heard this question from out of the blue, I thought I would first find out who he was before answering his question.

"Where are you from? What's your name?" I asked.

"Do you need to know my whereabouts before you respond to my queries?"

The Amritapuri ashram is open to anyone and everyone. Even though a vast majority of the people are devotees of Amma, one can also see people from other religious faiths and even non-believers roaming around the ashram premises. Normally, the visitors respect the atmosphere, the basic etiquette and rules and regulations. So, behavior like this was unusual and unexpected.

This could have easily turned into an unpleasant encounter. I ordered my mind to 'keep mum' and remembered the scriptural dictum, *'Athithi Devo Bhava*, Guest is God.' I should treat him accordingly. In any case, I mentally admired his audacity because this encounter took place in front of the main prayer hall of Amritapuri, which was then packed with devotees.

For some time, neither one of us spoke. Then my guest said, "My name is … I'm from … I have come here for an investigation."

"What are you investigating?"

"I want to know if God is here." The contempt and scorn in his words and tone were unmistakable.

I responded, "God is everywhere, not just here. In truth, I believe there's nothing that is not divine either here or there or anywhere."

"Isn't that merely an irrational belief?"

"Perhaps. What's your rational opinion?" I asked.

"That there is no God. There's no such power. I believe in reasoning, not in superstitions."

"Isn't that also a belief because you said, 'I believe in reasoning?' Where is the logic in merely saying, 'There's no such power?' However, I should say that our thoughts have something in common: we are both believers, aren't we?"

"We might be. But there's a big difference between us," the guest pointed out.

"Even so, the fact is that there is no existence without faith. You have to believe in something, right?"

"It does not matter. The fact that you are a God believer and I am an avowed atheist indicates a huge difference between us."

"But both of us are human beings. And humanness is common to us." I continued, "Friend, may I ask you something? In my understanding, 'atheism' is neither a lack of faith nor a denial of God. It's a perspective regarding the existence of divinity that transcends our mental powers, or, in other words, a supreme power. However, the first thing you said was, 'I want to know if God is here.'

Doesn't this mean that you cannot totally refute the existence of God? If someone knows that there is no God, why would he want to be here in the name of an investigation on that very topic?"

I do not know if it was because my answer touched a raw nerve, but the man suddenly became angry. "Are you telling me to leave?"

"Forgive me. I never intended that. If you feel that way, I apologize. I merely expressed a doubt on the subject of our conversation."

But my words had provoked him greatly. "Is this what your religious beliefs and faith in God amount to? Is this how Amma has taught you to behave?"

I replied, "Amma teaches us to become humane. I am extremely sorry that my words have hurt you so much."

I tried to appease him in many ways. I apologized numerous times. However, his anger did not abate. I could not understand why he was so furious. Then, without further ado, the two of us parted.

The next episode of this incident took place in the courtyard of the Calicut Brahmasthanam Temple.

There was hardly an inch of standing space, so huge was the crowd. Amma was meeting her children individually. She was doling out mercy, stealing glances, and pouring out the nectar of compassion to all in equal measure. I stood a short distance away, on one side of the stage, watching a 'darshan' that is uniquely Amma's.

There was an outpouring of hearts towards her. Some were shedding tears of joy in the rapture of pure devotion. Others had become still, absorbed in a meditative space. Some were lost in supreme joy. In yet others, the dams of sorrow had broken, releasing a deluge of tears. Amma was drawing everything and everyone to her maternal bosom. Her universal motherhood reminds one of the infinite ocean of supreme love.

While observing all this, I noticed a man paying his respects to Amma by touching her feet. With utmost devotion, he leaned on Amma's shoulder. Then, raising his head, he said something to her, prostrated again, stretched out both his hands to receive Amma's prasad, and then disappeared into the crowd of people. As I was closely watching Amma's darshan, I recognized him immediately; he was the 'atheist' I had seen in Amritapuri!

I quickly went to where the CCTV monitors were. Out of curiosity and to reassure myself, I looked at what had been recorded by the cameras. I had not forgotten his face. Yes, it was, indeed, that man…

But what gave me pause was something else. Was there some hidden motive to his coming here to see Amma? He was not so foolish as to think that no one would spot him or identify him in the crowd. It would not have been difficult for him to guess that I would be here. Then, what had happened between the time we met in Amritapuri and now? I was anxious to know. But whom to ask…?

About one-and-a-half or two hours must have passed. Darshan was still going on. I heard someone knocking on my door. When I opened the door, I saw a volunteer standing there. "Swamiji, someone is here to see you." Even before he could complete the sentence, the visitor appeared in front of me — my very own atheist! I was unable to hide my astonishment. It must have been the look on my face that prompted him to smile broadly. I noticed that there was a change in him.

"How are things? What brings you here…" I asked.

"I came to see Amma."

While I was wondering how to begin and what to ask, he started speaking again. "I'm sure you'll remember meeting me in Amritapuri and the circumstances when we parted. Before leaving that day, I spent a lot more time there. While roaming the ashram grounds, a man suddenly came to me and asked, 'Have you come to see Amma for the first time? Then you can go for darshan at once.'

"I decided that this was an opportunity to meet the 'Universal Mother' personally and question her. I accompanied the man to where Amma was seated. There were other people in front of me waiting for darshan. Finally, I was right in front of Amma. However, she did not embrace me like she does everyone. Before I could open my mouth to ask her the questions I had prepared, Amma laughed and said, 'Son, whether or not God exists might be moot. But no one can deny that there are people suffering in the world, right? Serving and loving them — this is the actual meaning of God. Amma is ever ready to wash the feet of one who selflessly serves the world, and to happily drink that sacred water, no matter who it is. More than the devotee anointed with sacred marks, Amma prefers the one without such a mark, but who loves others selflessly.'

The man went on to explain, "I felt as if a bolt of lightning had struck me somewhere inside. I was dumbstruck. Nothing was working—not my tongue, power of speech, nor my mind. Even then, Amma was looking at me and smiling. Some moments passed. I slowly got up and left.

"I walked until I reached the parking lot behind the ashram. It was deserted. Standing under an expansive sky, I felt as if a pleasant breeze was blowing both within me and outside. It was as if someone had pushed open a door that had remained closed for years...

"After this incident, I came to the ashram one more time to confess everything to Amma and beg her for forgiveness. I also wanted to meet you, Swamiji, but could not, because you were away. I still don't think of myself as a devotee. But Amma's words and her presence were able to create a transformation within me. They prevail as an incomparable, unforgettable and irresistible power within me that cannot be pushed aside or forgotten."

He ended his explanation with a long sigh, and then, becoming emotional, my friend clasped both my hands tightly and brought them close to his chest. "I don't claim to be a devotee, nor do I think I have any faith in miracles. However, I personally think that it would be irrational on my part if I don't accept a person such as Amma. I would have to be utterly stupid to deny a unique person such as her. I would be dishonest to my conscience if I didn't acknowledge this great giver, a giver of pure love, a listener par excellence, who does all this right in front of my eyes..." And he left.

While I watched him retreat into the distance, his heartfelt words continued to reverberate in my mind.

Amma's life and presence bring to mind the depth and expanse of an ocean that welcomes all rivers, giving them all equal importance.

The 'heart' is the center-point of the human body. We could also call it 'conscience.' The mind is filled with impurities and is home to innumerable emotions and thoughts. The heart or conscience is the substratum of all these.

As far as modern medical science is concerned, the heart is merely an organ that pumps blood to different parts of the body. In contrast, the scriptures regard it as the seat of the soul. The heart symbolizes the yearning to know the supreme power latent in us, to realize God as an incessant meditative effort and to imbibe this wisdom. The heart represents the love and longing of the individual soul to surrender to the supreme being and to merge with it. These are the range of meanings the word 'heart' implies in spiritual discourse.

For instance, there are moments in my life when my whole being opens up. This happens especially when I sing bhajans for Amma. Sometimes it is as if my heart is going to explode. It is a spiritually uplifting experience. My heart overflows with love. It is divine intoxication. No words can truly describe this feeling. This experience can happen to all those who consider work to be worship. If you closely observe such moments of inexplicable joy, you will find the source as the left side of your chest where the physical organ called the heart is located.

Why is Amma the Mother of the Universe? Because in her presence we experience the fullness of the heart, the very center of the universe. The subjective experience of God and God's divine qualities, such as love, purity, peace, compassion, bliss and equal vision, expresses itself as reality. Amma's physical presence and actions are proof that moksha, the highest state of human existence as described in the Vedas and Upanishads, is not a myth, but a true experience. Amma and her divine qualities bring to life the powerful concept of 'Jagadamba' (Mother of the Universe) as described in the Hindu faith.

That is why Amma is the Mother of all. Her all-embracing divine motherhood is, indeed, the power of Amma's irresistible attraction.

# 11 | EVER ESTABLISHED IN SAHAJA SAMADHI

Is there anyone in this world who doesn't meditate? If you say no, your answer would sound farfetched, but it would be the truth.

When we are hungry, we meditate on food. When we are sleepy, no other thought occupies the mind; forgetting time and place, we meditate on and summon the Goddess of Sleep! No need to mention the single-mindedness of the thief who has set out to steal. Or a baby who meditates on its mother's milk. The one-pointed focus of the predator stalking its prey is also a form of

meditation! Well-known, too, is the 'meditation' of the stork as it remains motionless in order to catch fish swimming in the shallows. Similarly, plants and trees also meditate, though we may not be aware of it.

Meditation is natural to our Being, our inner Self.

The essence and substratum of meditation is love. When we contemplate things, people and places we like, doesn't our mind become one with them? Meditation is the unbroken stream of thought on one object. However, when the feeling of love becomes involved, meditation evolves into spiritual ecstasy, thus acquiring a different dimension.

What happens to the lover when ruminating in solitude on the sweet memories of a delectable love? His mood and imagination become intense. His eyes close effortlessly. He forgets everything else, even if only for a few moments, and attains a state of absorption. Even though he does not plumb the depths of meditation, it is nevertheless a meditative experience.

When most people refer to 'love,' they allude merely to a purely physical and emotional experience. Actually, there is no love in it, only lust. And yet, one cannot categorically say, "It's not love!" In Amma's words, "It is the lowest level of love, like the bottom rung of a ladder. Instead of remaining there, one should use it to move upward. When we do so, that love gradually transforms into meditation."

The body's six centres — from the muladhara to the *ajna chakra*[9] — described in *Kundalini Yoga* are, in fact, not parts of the body perceptible to the eye. They are symbolic depictions of dormant spiritual power. They are also an ultra-subtle science and an inner experience.

The energy of love is unquestionable. It is the purest form of energy that an ordinary person can experience. However, its potential depends on its purity. The purer the love, the greater is its capacity.

---

9  Chakra = wheel; refers to the nerve plexuses or psychic centers of consciousness; there are a total of seven chakras located along the spinal cord, from the base to the cranial chamber. The muladhara chakra is located at the base of the spine, the ajna chakra between the eyebrows, and the sahasrara chakra, envisaged as a thousand-petalled lotus, at the top of the head.

The love one feels at the level of the body and emotions abides in the *muladhara* (the lowest of the six chakras). Ordinarily, there are two possibilities for love at that level. It can ascend to the highest level of existence. Or, as is the case with most people, it can remain at the lowest level, the circle of base emotions created by the body and mind.

The lotus enjoys an eminent position in Hindu iconography. It is an evergreen and charming symbol of abundance, beauty, spiritual success and eternity. Anyone would stop to gaze at this flower, which, though emerging from mire, exudes a pristine glory.

The ethereal beauty of the lotus is a metaphor for the spiritual evolution of the love that is ensnared in the muladhara chakra by sensuousness. The pink lotus, which blossoms from the mud, is an emblem of the seeker's spiritual pilgrimage and progress from the muladhara to the thousand-petalled lotus of the *sahasrara* (the highest point of spiritual existence).

The muladhara marks one extreme of existence. When the love dwelling therein is purified and transformed through tapas, it progresses

to the other extreme, the thousand-petalled sahasrara. Thus, lust, the lowest form of energy,
transforms into the highest, most powerful and
purified form of energy, which is unconditional
love. It is this blooming that one sees in the lotus.

Since the ultimate spiritual awakening is
inconceivable to the mind or the intellect, the
ancient seers used the symbol of the flowering
lotus, which emerges from the mud, and rises
from dirt to dignity, from lowliness to loftiness.
It is a subjective experience. Perhaps, the closest
metaphor the sages could come up with was the
opening of a bud to a fully blossomed flower. The
word *'sahasra'* in the scriptures denotes infinity.
So, the *sahasra-dala-padma* (the thousand petaled
lotus) signifies the experience of infinite Brahman,
oneness with the totality, thereby returning to
your original state of infinite bliss.

The fact is, meditation is the highest state of
love. When one attains that lofty state, love undergoes a metamorphosis; it becomes formless.

When the desire to realize God becomes an
acute and blazing inner pain, love becomes purified in the fire of that longing. The intensity of
that longing is the same as tapas. As the depth

and pervasiveness of love increases, it becomes a sheer presence, transcending all boundaries. That is what Amma means when she says, "I am love, the essence of love."

Once, someone asked Amma, "Are love and meditation different?"

Amma gave the following answer: "Those who think that love and meditation are two different things haven't understood the depth and meaning of either. When love deepens, it naturally becomes meditation. Love is the power that helps the flower of meditation grow, blossom and spread its fragrance everywhere. First, desire-based love should become selfless love. Gradually, it moves from worship of God with attributes to worship of the Formless Divine. In that state, you behold everything as God's glory and beauty. The world becomes God."

The word 'meditation' is etymologically derived from the Latin 'mederi,' which means to heal. Words like 'medicine,' 'medical,' 'meditate' and 'medicate' are all derived from 'mederi.'

We need medicines to heal the diseases that afflict the body. Similarly, meditation is necessary to heal the maladies of the mind.

Actually, to expedite healing, along with the medicines we take to cure the diseases of the body, it would be good if we could meditate also. If we understood the link between medicine and meditation, the course of treatment that doctors prescribe would change drastically. Perhaps this is the meaning of the old Malayalam adage 'medicine and mantra.' Medicine, of course, means proper treatment by a qualified doctor and the medications prescribed. Add *mantra japa* (repeated chanting of a mantra), and you have the divine formula that truly heals.

To subdue the mind, gain peace, and attain the goal of spirituality through meditation, one must become as patient and forbearing as the earth. The patient lying on a sickbed cannot afford to be impatient. Patience is absolutely necessary for healing. Impatience can lead to adverse consequences.

There are two types of diseases: physical and mental. Poor physical health can be healed with medicine, and poor mental health can be healed through meditation.

In order to conquer the peaks of materialism and spirituality, one must love one's chosen field of activity. We must embrace it wholeheartedly.

"The power of love acts like a booster rocket, and meditation takes one to the peak," says Amma.

Some scientists and artists of prodigious intellectual powers are known to have experienced this state of meditation. When we read the works of certain great poets and writers, we feel as if the secrets of the universe have been unveiled to them, so lofty was their vision. Unfortunately, apart from a rare few, most of them fall an easy victim to the temptations of their mind and indulge uncontrollably, thus ruining their own lives.

When dancers dance, when singers sing, and when musicians play their instruments, they seem to glide into a state of meditative absorption. However, none of them can remain established in that state or enter the realm of unending bliss. They may remain in the state of inner absorption for some time. After that, they slip again into normal mental conflicts and agitations. This is one reason why meditation is important. As Amma says, "Just as we eat and sleep, meditation and spiritual practices should also become an indispensable part of our daily routine."

As mentioned earlier, love's intensity increases the depth of meditation and makes it whole.

When meditation becomes a means of mental purity and spiritual liberation, the love on which it is predicated becomes transformed. It becomes capable of leading the seeker to the highest levels of existence. Amma says, "When meditation becomes like an unbroken stream, an incessant flow, at that point, you experience total oneness with the whole."

Amma is the highest state of meditation. The stillness, bliss and beauty of meditation are evident in all her activities. If we observe Amma with all our heart, that experience will become clear to us. Gradually, we can become rightful heirs to the same experience. The best place to imbibe the essence of meditation and to become meditation itself is in the holy presence of a Satguru such as Amma.

Amma says, "A cold climate is necessary to cultivate apple trees and for them to bear fruit. They won't grow in Kerala. If they do, they won't bear much fruit, nor will they be tasty or sweet as apples where this fruit grows naturally. Yet, apple trees will grow abundantly in Kashmir, as the climate there is conducive. Similarly, a Satguru's presence is the ideal and best 'climate' for sadhaks who wish to practice meditation and grow spiritually."

It is worthwhile to meditate on Amma's words, "When the mind dissolves in true meditation, there is no return. Once the mind is established therein, one becomes the very heart of the universe. Everything becomes 'I.' 'I' pervades every place. One begins to attract everything. One obtains everything. One becomes a mere presence capable of uplifting all, a loving presence that touches all beings like a flowing river or a passing breeze."

*Sahaja samadhi* is the supreme state of existence where one is fully established in the unalterable experience of oneness with Brahman. Amma is the glorious and abundant presence of the ingrained wisdom of perfection in meditation and compassion. Her form and touch, sound and silence, taciturnity and eloquence, food and sleep, play and laughter, love and anger, gaze and movement are all meditation, the continuing manifestation of sahaja samadhi.

# 12 | THE ALL-ENCOMPASSING NATURE OF THE GURU

Amritapuri is ever blissful. It celebrates Guru Purnima incessantly, owing to the presence of perfection in the form of Amma. Every moment with Amma is Guru Purnima. Her presence casts the glow of Self-knowledge on earth. Every sand particle and air molecule in Amritapuri carries the vibrations of great festivity. A sliver of that Knowledge must have illumined Sri Ottoor Unni Namboothirippad's heart, for the very first mantra of Amma's *Ashtottaram* (108 attributes) he composed was *'Om purna -brahma-svarupinyai namah'*— Salutations to her, who is the complete manifestation of the Supreme.

A Satguru is indeed an embodiment of the Supreme. Guru Purnima is a day when the disciple devoutly and worshipfully remembers the guru's sublime glory and all-pervading nature.

The 15th century Indian mystic poet, Kabir, depicts the greatness of the Satguru, proclaiming, "The guru is great beyond words, and great is the good fortune of the disciple." He sang the glory

of the guru thus: "It is the mercy of my true guru that has led me to know the unknown. I have learned from him how to walk without feet, to see without eyes, to hear without ears, to drink without a mouth, to fly without wings. I have brought my love and my meditation into the land where there is no sun and moon, nor day and night. Without eating, I have tasted the sweetness of nectar. Without water, I have quenched my thirst. Where there is the response of delight, there is the fullness of joy. Before whom can that joy be uttered?"

For the disciple, the guru is everything. The guru's form and limitless compassion are objects of the disciple's meditation. There is no other place that his mind and intellect can go. Disciples who have attained such heights are rare. They are a wonder.

Amma says, "Spirituality is a return journey to our true source of emergence. It is part of our evolutionary process that each one of us will have to embark upon at some point, either in this life or subsequent lives." To those who ask, "When?" Amma says, "Now. Here. This moment is best suited for striving to attain that realization.

Waiting for the thoughts to subside before commencing one's spiritual inquiry is like expecting the waves to stop before swimming in the ocean. One must turn within and begin Self-inquiry the moment the inquisitiveness to know the truth about existence dawns."

Once we meet a Satguru, once that human manifestation of universal consciousness appears in our lives, we must tarry no longer, for there is nothing greater than that in human life. Don't doubt; don't allow the mind to corrupt your longing.

As soon as the thought arises, "I must pursue my spiritual practices without further delay," we must not waste even a moment getting started. The mind is fickle. Thoughts move at the speed of the wind.

In the *Bhagavad Gita*, the great warrior Arjuna asks Lord Krishna:

> *cañcalam hi manaḥ kṛṣṇa pramāthi*
> *balavaddṛḍham*
> *tasyāham nigraham manyē vāyōriva*
> *suduṣkaram*

The mind is very restless, turbulent, strong and obstinate, O Krishna. It appears to me that it is more difficult to control than the wind. (6.34)

For his disciple's sincere doubt, Krishna recommends a two-pronged solution. He suggests *'abhyasa'* (constant practice) and *'vairagya'* (an attitude of non-attachment with proper discernment) as ways to tame and discipline the mind.

How does one achieve excellence in a given area of work, be it art, science, business, politics or any other subject? Continuous practice, right? It is like someone who has mastered karate. Once you have mastered it, there is no more effort; even the most complicated movements simply flow through you. You don't even have to think. It just happens. But to accomplish that spontaneity, you need years of continuous and deliberate practice. Eminent people, artists, singers, musicians and athletes all practice their art for hours on end every day without fail.

Amma gives a striking example of vairagya. She says, "Suppose you are allergic to wheat or milk products. Wouldn't you refrain from eating pizza, chappatis, or ice-cream, when all your friends have ordered one of these items in a restaurant? This understanding comes from the realization that consuming wheat or milk products can cause you a severe allergic reaction, right? In a like manner, a sadhak should develop a distaste for worldly pleasures, knowing they are harmful for his spiritual growth."

What happens if someone is engaged in non-stop running? He or she will get tired, exhausted and will ultimately collapse, right? We should take a moment to watch our own life. What are we doing? We are running a race, physically, mentally and emotionally, correct? That is why it is known as the 'rat race' — a way of life in modern society in which people compete with each other for power and money.

We need to allow our consciousness to expand. How do we expand our consciousness? Amma says, "In reality there is no expansion or contraction for consciousness. It is ever full and unchangeable. But, as long as we are identified with the body and mind, there is a so-called expansion in our consciousness. This takes place through small acts of kindness, compassion, heartfelt smiles, beautiful and touching words, understanding others, forgetting, forgiving and through spiritual practices such as meditation, japa, etc."

In everyday life, we are in a continuous process of 'doing' and 'undoing.' We don't see it. Thus, we are unaware of it. Don't we have to undo many things we have been doing as part of our life for so long? We move from one city to another, from an old house to a new house, from a familiar neighborhood to an unfamiliar one, from one office or job environment to a new one. All minor and major transitions in life involve giving up some of our old habits and learning new ones. This is known as abhyasa.

We do possess the inner capacity to develop spiritual qualities, provided we have the earnestness and enthusiasm to do so. This process also involves vairagya, because, while moving from one situation to embrace another, we should also detach ourselves from the former. Looking at life from this angle, we are constantly practicing abhyasa and vairagya. When your goal is God realization, the attitude and the intensity of this process also has to be increased.

The thought wave arising in the present moment will be overcome by the waves that follow. An endless evolutionary process takes place within us, wherein the roaring future pushes the present into the oblivion of the past. Such is the mind. Therefore, if we do not act on noble impulses at once, they will lose their force and we might well lose a golden opportunity to dive into the depths of our own Self.

Spirituality is the search for one's own reality, and the subject of study is one's own Self. There is nothing greater in this world than knowing one's Self. It involves owning the totality of universal existence. When the mind becomes purified through tapas, the awareness that "I am God; I am All" is unveiled. With the dawn of Self-knowledge, one transcends likes and dislikes. Notions of 'inside' and 'outside' fade away. One experiences within the infinity of *maha-akash* ('great space,' i.e. universal consciousness).

However, those who wish to pursue the path must prepare themselves to receive this highest knowledge. When the seeker develops the readiness to prepare, to be ever vigilant, the Satguru appears. Until then, you will not experience the

Satguru, even if she is physically present in your life. That is what Amma means when she says, "First, there must be a disciple. Only then will there be a guru." The disciple's total willingness to be disciplined is most important. The Satguru's sole aim is to wake you up from the deep slumber of ignorance. Thus, if you feel "fired up" in the presence of a Satguru, take it as a good sign. That means, the guru has started working on you.

Being a disciple demands constant preparation. Actually, our whole life is a kind of non-stop preparation. The moment the umbilical cord is severed, each one of us begins a lifelong preparation to live a happy and peaceful life in this world. Nevertheless, a close observation of people all over the world reveals that they gather much disappointment and frustration during their life time, which ultimately results in immense grief. The irony is that even though we are continuously preparing to live, we never actually live life. Don't we hear people on their deathbed say, "Throughout my entire life I only prepared to live, but I never lived." Therefore, the practice of spirituality, based on the principles of unburdening and letting go of your unintelligent attachments, is important.

There is a story about a very wealthy man who was immensely attached to his riches. So, it was natural he wished to live for a thousand years. He visited many sacred places and consulted many holy men hoping to fulfil his wish. Once, while on a pilgrimage, someone told him that there was an ancient cave in the Himalayas, inside of which was a small stream flowing with water that could significantly increase his lifespan. He immediately went there and found the stream. The man was ecstatic. He happily cupped its water and was about to drink. Suddenly he heard a voice, "Don't do it. Think deeply before you drink the water." The man looked around. It was a crow. The man asked the bird, "Why? Do you have a justification for your argument?" The crow said, "Yes, I do. I drank the water from the stream once. Now, my life goes on and on. However, I am totally unhappy and discontent." The crow continued, "I have seen everything in life, experienced everything — name, fame, power, love, success, failure and so forth. I was the king of the crow community. I have had many wives, so many children... you name it, I had it. Now I am fed up and somehow want to end this life, but I can't. I even tried to commit suicide. That also failed because I have to wait until I exhaust the predetermined period of my life. My friend, to be very honest with you, I am suffering tremendously, beyond words. So, please consider my request and don't drink the water." It is said that the wealthy man understood the reality about life, and he left the cave without consuming the water. This story is a metaphor to show that anything outside of you can be a source of pain at any given point of time. Even a long lifespan will not end your suffering as unintelligent attachment is bound to create disturbance in your natural state of peace and tranquillity.

This does not mean that we shouldn't have any desires or possessions. We certainly can, but don't let them possess you. This is the secret of living a happy life. The moment you try to grab and make it your own, you will be pulled off center, the symphony of your life will become a melancholic dirge. A Satguru's job is to bring back the symphony and eventually pave the path for us to reach the state of transcendence. But for this, we should have the willingness to let the guru work on our likes and dislikes. The guru is always ready, but unless we allow, the guru won't start the work.

I have heard many people tell Amma, "I never had this problem before, but since I started meditating, endless thoughts come. Why is this?" The answer is, because we never tried to meditate and silence the mind before. Meditation is like bringing light to a pitch-dark room. When we light a lamp, everything in the room becomes visible. Likewise, when meditation silences the mind, we see the dormant negative emotions. It is not that meditation created new thoughts and emotions. It just helped you see what has always been there.

The direct guidance and divine presence of a Satguru gives us insight into the various aspects of spiritual sadhana, including the much needed flexibility in performing one's sadhana, irrespective of time and place.

Some people say, "I can only meditate if I am in a forest or in one of the Himalayan caves." This is also attachment, an obstacle on the path to God realization. Allow me to quote Amma. She says, "No matter where you are, you should be able to meditate. All the 24 hours should be perfectly under your control."

The nature of our inner Self is peace and silence. However, the mind is opposed to this. Its nature is to create turbulence and disharmony. As a result, the moment we try to return to a peaceful state, the mind interferes. Thoughts and emotions gush in. Turbulence is unnatural to the Self. It is the same with water when it boils. Its normal state is stillness. Water wants to retain its original state, so it becomes agitated when boiled.

Basically, it is not an object, person, or situation that triggers disturbance in the mind. It is not even a physical or psychological relationship. None of these aspects are capable of activating any pain. Don't we feel sad or heartbroken about something that occurs in a faraway place, perhaps, on the other side of the world, a disaster that happens to a country or to a group of people? Do we have any physical relationship there? No. So, it is not the relationship itself that is the cause of the sadness pain. The real cause is our wrong perception of the world and its objects.

The world is in a constant flux. Change is an inevitable law. Therefore, attachment to something or someone will soon be overtaken by aversion. When you like something or someone, dislike is waiting just around the corner to overpower you. Therefore, our great rishis advised us to rise above the emotions and become centered in our Being, our true Self.

Just before the Kurukshetra War began, Arjuna was blessed with the unprecedented good fortune of seeing Lord Krishna's cosmic form. Just imagine that blessed moment! That exceptional vision was God's response to `a unique situation. That unworldly moment took Arjuna to the heights of wonder and fear, and finally helped him beg forgiveness for all his mistakes and surrender totally to the Lord.

> *yaccāvahāsārtham asat-kṛtō'si*
> *vihāra-śayyāsana-bhōjanēṣu*
> *ekō'tha vāpy acyuta tat-samakṣam*
> *tat kṣāmayē tvām aham apramēyam*

> And if, in a jestful manner, I treated you with disrespect, while playing, resting, sitting, eating, when alone, or before others—for all that I crave forgiveness. (*Bhagavad Gita*, 11.42)

At that moment, Arjuna no longer saw the Krishna who had been his charioteer until a moment ago and whom he had considered an equal, a friend who laughed and played and chatted with him, and with whom he had experienced both the closeness and conflicts that are part and parcel of friendship. In that blessed moment, Arjuna beheld before him the Almighty in human form. The 11th chapter of the *Bhagavad Gita* elaborately describes this astonishing marvel: "With innumerable mouths and eyes, a myriad of wonderful sights, a full array of celestial ornaments, and heavenly weapons uplifted…" (10)

It was as if nature had acquired countless tongues, and each atom and each blade of grass were addressing Arjuna in one voice. Through these tongues, Arjuna was able to grasp the secret of dharma.

The *vishva-rupa darshan* (vision of the cosmic form) is God's dialogue with man, a message from the totality of cosmic powers, and the universal guru's counsel to the disciple. To understand the meaning of the words uttered by great gurus, knowledge of Sanskrit alone is insufficient. One must go beyond words. Their every word, full stop, comma and semicolon are worthy of meditation, as they are all imbued with their sanctifying breath.

The term 'gravitational force' is generally used to denote the earth's power to attract. The earth does nothing in particular, and yet, everything is drawn to it. What one experiences in the Satguru's presence is something similar: it is the attraction towards the guru's all-encompassing nature. This lure is indescribable, invisible, heartfelt and charming.

The guru is leading the disciple to the mystic source of the universe's infinite power. For this very reason, her method of teaching may not conform to ordinary knowledge and logic. The disciple must possess the maturity to receive the teachings, free from preconceptions. The guru will completely upend the disciple's notions and beliefs. She will shatter the disciple's ideas about the world, life and relationships. In that process of re-creation, one may feel at times that the guru's compassion is merciless!

Aren't teachers strict with their pupils at times if they sincerely want their students to study well, have a bright future, attain high positions, and discharge their duties with an attitude of surrender? That strictness is nothing but a mask concealing the teachers' deep love and care for the pupils. If we cannot discern the sincere intentions of even ordinary teachers who teach material subjects, how can we fathom the modus operandi of a Satguru as she tries to prepare the disciple to realize the Supreme Self?

Like the vast expanse of the sky, the Satguru is purely a presence. Here, the teaching is not done through pressure or force. Nothing will happen without the disciple's full consent, his utter receptivity and self-surrender.

Self-realization is the pinnacle of bliss. Once immersed in that ocean of sat-chit-ananda, there is no return. In that non-dual state, one might not feel love and compassion for the world or its people. But rare souls do return, like our beloved Amma, who is by nature an ocean of mercy. They come back to uplift the world, to offer succour to the suffering and to guide seekers of Truth. They flow like a Ganges of love and compassion. They live among ordinary people as one among them but work with extraordinary ability. They are Satgurus, the divine incarnations.

Even when the earth is bathed in moonlight, even when that light comforts the body and consoles the mind, man still points to the shadows of imperfections on the full moon. Likewise, out of ignorance, we, too, find fault with the full moon of the guru's unflawed presence, purity and divine light.

The guru is the embodiment of patience and will wait indefinitely for the disciple to open his/her heart. However, those who wish to become disciples must have a clear understanding of their own life—what they really want. "What is my real path? Do I have the maturity and wisdom to become a *sannyasi* (ascetic who has renounced the world) directly after *brahmacharya* (phase of life characterized by spiritual study)? Or, is it my dharma to become a householder, then pass through *vanaprastha* (withdrawal from worldly responsibilities) and then lead the life of a sannyasi? One who is on the spiritual path should sincerely pose these questions inwardly and find the answers. I am reminded of Lord Krishna's words in the *Bhagavad Gita*:

> *caturvidhā bhajantē mām janāḥ*
> *sukṛtinō'rjuna*
> *ārtō jijñāsur arthārthī jñānī ca*
> *bharataṛṣhabha*

> O Arjuna, best among men, four types
> of people worship Me: the distressed, the
> seeker of knowledge, the seeker of wealth,
> and the wise. (7.16).

Some people seek God's help only when they fall sick, when examinations draw near, or when they are hard-pressed for money, etc. They are the *aarthas* (the distressed seeking fulfilment of their desires). Then there are those who study subjects such as history, geography, music and literature, and out of curiosity, might peek into the subject of God as well. Such people belong to the second category of devotees: *jijnaasus* (seekers of knowledge). Yet another category is the *arthaarthis* (seekers of wealth). They want wealth but wish to earn it righteously, for their goal is spiritual liberation. In contrast to the other three categories, the *jnaanis* (wise) do not wish for anything other than knowing God.

Before preparing to become a disciple, it would be good to contemplate the advice that Lord Krishna gave Arjuna. One should ask oneself, "To which of these categories do I belong?" and find the answer. The Lord is not partial to any among these four groups. That said, the jnani is closer to God by virtue of his thoughts, deeds and attitude.

In fact, Lord Krishna was not partial towards the Pandavas or prejudiced against the Kauravas. To think that he was would be a mistake. The Lord, who was a Satguru and who had equal vision, was beyond likes and dislikes. In his universal mind, friend and foe, noble and evil all had an equal place. There is no place whatsoever for such distinctions, as the entire cosmos exists in the maha-akash, which is the true nature of the Satguru. The universe arises from that infinitude, exists in it, and will dissolve in it eventually.

The Pandavas took refuge in Lord Krishna. Even during the Mahabharata War, their sole request was that Lord Krishna be on their side, even if unarmed. Though the Lord had no enemies, the Kauravas saw him as one. Krishna could not be blamed for that. It was a problem with the minds and attitudes of the Kauravas. If the Lord was prejudiced against the Kauravas, would he have given them his million-strong Narayani Army of chivalrous soldiers? Has such a thing ever happened in world history?

If embodied, one must live in this world. This is also the case with Satgurus. However, their level of awareness transcends the whole universe. Lord Krishna graced this earth with his presence 5,000 years ago, whereas Amma is living here with us now. Ages may pass, but the source of the level of awareness in which Satgurus abide and the words they utter is one. Amma abides in the very same supreme level of awareness in which Lord Krishna was established.

Just as Lord Krishna, Amma, too, descended from that supreme realm of awareness to this world, solely out of her boundless compassion for the suffering and for spiritual seekers who have dedicated their life to God-realization. 'Boundless compassion' is the only reason for them to assume a human form, work in our midst, and be a tremendous source of inspiration for us. There is no other explanation.

When sat-chit-ananda assumes a human form, descends to earth, and flows as the Ganges of Amrita (immortality), some swim in it; some bathe in it; some drink from it; and some spit into it. One's behavior depends on one's level of discernment and rectitude. Not that the river cares. It can only flow and will continue flowing. No one can stop that perennial flow from Amritapuri to the rest of the world. Living with Amma is the same as living with God...

# 13 | TORRENTIAL GRACE

"Though the sun is far away in the sky, the lotus flowers on earth still blossom. In a like manner, where there is love, distance is no barrier." These are Amma's words. Those who revel only in the world of logic and the intellect will find it hard to fathom the depth of this analogy. But the unfurling of the heart-lotus and the experience of its unearthly beauty and fragrance are not unfamiliar to those whose hearts have known the shower of pure love. My life has been an unending succession of such wondrous experiences.

Let me share one such experience, which took place at the end of Amma's 2017 Japan-North America Tour. Whether in India or elsewhere, Amma travels by road from one place to another. A fleet of buses containing hundreds of devotees accompanies her. Amma was scheduled to visit the city of Toronto, Canada, for four days, during which we would celebrate Guru Purnima. Afterwards, Amma and the tour group would return to India. Many devotees were coming from all parts of the US and Canada to Toronto for Guru Purnima.

No matter where in the world we may be, there will be a stop in the evening for tea and supper. This constant in Amma's tours is known as the 'chai stop.' While travelling across India, such stops can be anywhere: solitary places or parks, by the roadside or near gas stations, or in fields or playgrounds. In the west, these stops will be in designated areas such as a public park. There, Amma will sit with her children. Meditation will be the first thing, followed by devotional singing, a Q&A session and prayers for world peace. Quite often, Amma will also request the little children travelling with the group to tell stories and the

elders to speak on a chosen subject. Thereafter, Amma will serve food to everyone.

After her programs in Washington DC, Amma and the fleet of buses left for Toronto. Niagara Falls is about 10 minutes from the Canadian border. That year, we had the chai stop in a park immediately adjacent to Niagara Falls. On one side was Niagara Falls, one of the wonders of the world, and on the other was the glorious presence of the marvel known as Amma. The scriptures say that a Self-realized master is the greatest miracle.

After the usual round of chai stop activities, the tour group left for the Canadian border. Just as Amma's vehicle was about to move onto the road leading to the border, she suddenly said, for no apparent reason, "Please stop the vehicle. We can leave after a while." When I heard this, I felt some misgivings within.

"What is it, Amma?" I asked.

"Oh, nothing!" replied Amma.

Her tone of voice seemed to be hinting at something. I stepped out of the car. My mind started wondering, "Why would Amma ask us to stop the vehicle?" As I could not figure out anything from the prevailing circumstances, I stopped trying to find an explanation. From experience, I know that Amma alone is capable of understanding the meaning and significance of her words and actions, especially at times like these when she asked to stop the vehicle for no apparent reason.

While standing there, I felt that I should take out my passport, wherein my Canadian visa had been printed along with other relevant documents for clearing immigration. The Canadian visa was in my newest passport. As the visas to some other countries were in older passports, all the older passports had been bound together with the newest one.

To help me easily locate the visa for each country, I had pasted different-coloured Post-it Notes on the pages of the different visas. I turned to the page bearing the Canadian visa. When I checked it, I realized that it had expired in May that year, two months before. At first, I thought that I had pasted the Post-it Note on the wrong page. After all, it was already July. I went through each and every page of the three passports I had. All the Canadian visas I had were those that had expired in previous years. I checked and rechecked. I did not see a current visa.

The devotees travelling with us also examined my passports thoroughly. At last, it became apparent that I did not have a valid visa. I could not enter Canada.

The job of obtaining visas for the sannyasis travelling abroad with Amma is the responsibility of one particular brahmachari. There had been no lapse in this matter all these years. When I called him to tell him what had happened, he was terribly sorry and perplexed; he had no idea how that could have happened.

When the reality of the situation dawned on me, my first thought was, "I won't be able to perform *pada puja*, worship of Amma's feet, on Guru Purnima… My practice of doing so for 30+ years without fail would be broken…"

I informed Amma, who was sitting in the car, that I did not have a visa. "Son…" That was all she said. Her voice had all the concerns of a mother. Then, she slowly said, "Amma felt something wasn't right. That's why she suddenly asked for the vehicle to be stopped." No one said anything. "What will you do?" Amma asked.

My mind was numb. Dark clouds of pain began to fill my heart, waiting to burst. I gazed into Amma's eyes. "Amma understands her son's heart." This is what those eyes conveyed.

At this point, Gautam Harvey, an American who resides in Amritapuri, said, "Let's try anyway. Let us tell the officer everything. Who knows, he may help us find a way out."

I asked Amma for permission to go ahead. "Try." There was a shadow of doubt both in Amma's word and facial expression.

"Don't expect anything. Let's try our luck anyway," Gautam suggested.

We arranged another vehicle. I stood watching as Amma's car drove away. I felt that the tears I was holding back would soon gush forth. Suppressing my grief, I quickly got into the car. We soon reached the Canadian Immigration Office at the border. We explained matters. Sure enough, I was denied a visa and was ordered to return to the US.

Near the Canadian border is the American city of Buffalo. Bharat Jayaram, a professor at the university there, is a close devotee of Amma. We decided to stay in his house that night. When we reached his place, it was after 1:00 a.m. Bharat invited us to eat. I was still reeling from the shock of what had happened. I had been doing pada puja to Amma on Guru Purnima for the last three decades. I had not missed it even once. That practice was now going to be broken. With that pain raging inside me like a roaring inferno, how could I think about appeasing my pangs of hunger?

People familiar with immigration laws were of the opinion that I was unlikely to get a Canadian visa within two days. However, they agreed that there was nothing wrong with applying directly at the Canadian Consulate in New York. Amma also told me to do just that. I decided to take the first flight out to New York that next day. Sneha (Karen Moawad), who works on International Programs at Amrita University, agreed to fly to New York to try to help.

By the time I went to bed, it was past two in the morning. I had fallen into a state of despair. Tears would not stop flowing. My precious Amma was now in Toronto. The task to obtain a visa seemed insurmountable, especially as a weekend was coming. But I knew I had to make some effort if Amma's grace was to flow.

We purchased tickets to LaGuardia Airport instead of JFK in order to minimize the driving time to Manhattan once we arrived. It was a 30-minute drive from there to the Canadian Consulate. However, fate was not kind even then. Owing to stormy weather in New York, the Buffalo flight that was supposed to take off at 9:00 a.m. was delayed. Finally, the plane took off from Buffalo after 12:30 p.m. By the time we reached the Consulate, it was Friday after 3:00 p.m. The Canadian Consulate closes at 3:00 p.m. on Fridays. My last resort to obtain a visa had failed.

The Consulate would only open again the next Monday. By then, Amma's programs in Canada would have almost ended. While Sneha and I stood in front of the doors to the Consulate wondering what to do, a kind security officer, wanting very much to help us, told us that we should go to the visa agency across town, and that the agency was open until 5:00 p.m. We jumped in an Uber and raced to the agency. However, the visa agency could not promise they would have my passport back to me before the flight to India, so I opted not to apply there for the Canadian visa.

My over-riding goal was to get into Canada to be with Amma for Guru Purnima or at the very least to be able to fly into Toronto Tuesday in order to fly back to India with Amma.

It was obvious that staying in New York over the weekend would serve little purpose, but now we had missed the last flight back to Buffalo, so we spent the night in New York City. I could not close my eyes even for a second. At 2:30 a.m. the phone rang. It was Amma. Without any preamble, she said, "Son, return to Buffalo tomorrow morning. Gautam will be there, waiting to take you to the Canadian border. Try one more time. After all, we should make every attempt, shouldn't we? The rest is God's grace." She had called while giving darshan. Amma's words reminded me of the famous verse from the *Bhagavad Gita*.

> *karmaṇy-ēvādhikāras tē mā phalēṣu kadācana*
> *mā karma-phala-hētur bhūr mā tē sango'stvakarmaṇi*
>
> You have control and command only upon the activities but never on their results. You should not be the cause of the

result of activities. Do not be interested in getting dispensed with activities. (2.47)

Gautam called and explained to me that we were going to try for a TRP (temporary resident permit) to enter Canada. In rare cases, the immigration officers had the authority to issue a TRP. He reminded me that we had Amma's permission to proceed.

In the meantime, Gautam, with the help of the tour information group, was able to gather materials about Amma and my role at the Amrita University and Embracing the World, and so Sneha and I flew back to Buffalo to try another checkpoint at the border.

We left early that morning for Buffalo. Gautam was already waiting at Bharat Jayaram's home. By 10:00 a.m. we left for the Peace Bridge at the Canadian border. We drove up through one of the three lanes to a booth of the Canada Border Services Agency. The officer asked for my passport. While examining my documents, he politely asked, "Why were you denied a visa two days ago?" While candidly explaining what had happened, Gautam explained we now had additional documentation and inquired if there was any chance of my obtaining a temporary visa. The officer peered into the car, looked at me, and smiled. He then calmly and politely said, "I wouldn't say that it's impossible to obtain a temporary visa. However, there are many regulations pertaining to the issuing of such a visa. Many documents would need to be produced. So, it's very difficult to obtain such a visa."

I was bowled over by the officer's gentle tone and courteous manner. He asked us to go to the Immigration Office inside the nearby building.

There were many people there waiting for permission to enter Canada. I prayerfully joined them and waited for my turn.

Among those who had been denied a visa were a father and daughter. The father was trying to take his eight-year-old daughter with him to Canada. He was a divorcee. The immigration officer made it clear to him that, even though she was his daughter, she would not be granted a visa without a letter from the girl's mother. The father looked helpless, and the daughter stood there, not knowing what was happening.

A mother and her two children were sleeping on the bench. They were refugees. An immigration officer was nearby with food for them.

Time seemed to hardly move as I waited. After a while, my name was called. I humbly presented the officer with my passport and other documents. He looked stern. Barely glancing at the documents, the officer harshly said, "You knew very well that you needed a visa to travel to the United States. Didn't you know that you would also need a visa to enter Canada? Why, then, didn't you obtain one? I don't care who you are or how important you may be."

Unfortunately, this officer was the antithesis of the kind man outside. He flatly said, "You had time to get a U.S. visa, but you didn't bother to get a Canadian visa. If the program in Toronto can go on without you, I am not going to grant a visa." Finally, when we told him I had performed Guru Purnima for the last 32 years and that the ceremony might not happen if I were not to be able to perform it, he threw up his hands and said he would have someone else take over the case.

Matters were getting complicated. It seemed as if there was no hope.

We continued waiting. Within minutes, another officer arrived and took his seat next to the first officer. He called my name. When I reached the counter, I was pleasantly surprised; it was the courteous officer we had seen at the booth outside! I presented him with all the documents. He spent the next hour pouring over our materials. We waited anxiously, praying constantly to Amma.

"Mr. Puri!" When I heard my name being called, I went to the counter. What was he going to say? I looked at him anxiously. "I shall grant you a temporary visa. But only this time." He smiled. I could not believe my ears, but my heart whispered, "Grace... Amma's infinite grace!" He not only agreed to give a temporary visa, he extended it one day in case our flight from Canada was going to be delayed. We knew it was Amma who was working through this man.

All four of us took turns to thank that kind officer profusely. As our hearts were filled with elation, our eyes also overflowed with tears.

How many such experiences there have been, that cannot be analysed or explained! After leaving Niagara Falls, Amma asking us to stop the car for no apparent reason had been a hint. If not, I would have reached the border under the mistaken understanding that I had a valid visa. When Amma asked the car to be stopped, I had checked my passport. What if my passport had been checked later at the Immigration Office? I could even have been jailed for trying to 'deceive' the Immigration Office!

Some people wondered, "Couldn't Amma have let you know that you did not have a valid visa way before all this happened?" Such a doubt is not without merit. Lord Krishna knew all along that the Kurukshetra War was inevitable, right? Yet, why didn't he tell Arjuna that the war was destined to happen, no matter how much Krishna and the Pandavas tried to avert it?

In all experiences of life, not just this experience of mine, we cannot ignore two factors: the limited human intellect and the inscrutable ways of the universe. Reason and intelligence are necessary. However, life is not always amenable to human understanding. Some things will always remain a mystery. To understand and appreciate even a small part of the magnitude and complexity of how the universe works, what is needed is love and faith.

Human intelligence can explain many things. However, the underlying essence of life is a mystery. Perhaps, that is why Albert Einstein declared, "The most beautiful thing we can experience is the mysterious. It is the source of all true art and science. He to whom the emotion is a stranger, who can no longer pause to wonder and stand wrapped in awe, is as good as dead — his eyes are closed."

In the 11th chapter of the *Bhagavad Gita*, Lord Krishna reveals his cosmic form to Arjuna. The warrior beholds the entire universe, the animate and inanimate, the entire solar system, galaxies, heaven and hell existing in the Lord's body. The message of the cosmic form is that the individual has no separate existence from the totality.

Who can unearth the secrets that the indivisible universal power has hidden, in seed form, within us?

Amma says, "We can resolve some situations of life and certain others cannot be fixed, no matter how much we try. We must make maximum effort when we have the choice to solve a situation, and we must accept situations where we are left with no choice. For example, a person trying to add half a foot to his height may not succeed in his attempt, even if he hangs upside down the whole day, or takes various multivitamins. Here, the only choice is to accept and be happy with what you have. However, there are situations, such as failing in an interview, where you can appear and reappear for interviews until you get a job."

It has already been predetermined that certain incidents must take place in an individual's life, that he or she must undergo certain experiences. These are secrets hidden in the recesses of the universe's heart. No power can change this. No one can alter such predetermined matters. However, if one has the protection of a divine incarnation or Satguru, who has realized the universal power… 'what was supposed to hit the eye might graze the eyebrow instead.'

Karna, the ace archer, had released an arrow aimed at Arjuna's neck. Using his toe, Lord Krishna lowered the chariot, and the arrow knocked off Arjuna's crown, instead of striking his neck.

Amma abides in the same supreme state in which Krishna, Rama and the Buddha were established. Sri Ramakrishna Parmahamsa once told Swami Vivekananda, "Naren, (Narendranath was Swami Vivekananda's name before he took sannyasa) he who is Rama, he who is Krishna, in one form in this body is Ramakrishna."

Therefore, if someone asks, "Where are Krishna, Rama and the Buddha?" I would state categorically, without the slightest doubt whatsoever, "They dwell here in Amritapuri, in the form of Amma, who sees into the hearts of human beings."

Divine grace is a manifestation of the cosmic free will in operation. It can alter the course of events in a mysterious manner through its own unknown laws, which are superior to all the natural laws, and can modify the latter by interaction. It is the most powerful force in the universe. It descends and acts only when it is invoked by total self-surrender. It acts from within, because God resides in the heart of all beings. Its whisper can be heard only in a mind purified by self-surrender and prayer.

It is believed that sage Narada asked Lord Vishnu about the simplest sadhana to perform at the advent of Kali Yuga.

*nāham vasāmi vaikuṇṭhe yōgināṃ hṛdayē
na ca*
*madbhaktā yatra gāyanti tatra tiṣṭhāmi
nārada*

Neither do I reside in Vaikuntha (Lord Vishnu's abode) nor do I dwell in the hearts of the yogis, O Narada, I stay where my devotees sing.

Rationalists laugh at it and atheists scorn it, but it exists. Divine Grace is God's descent into the soul's zone of awareness.

# 14 | COME QUICKLY, DARLING CHILDREN

Of the many problems and limitations human beings have, one of them is that we can only perceive everything from the standpoint of an ordinary human being, even when we view God. Whenever we talk about God, we call Him or Her the all-pervasive, ever-present and all-knowing infinite power. Some judge God as being partial, cruel, the cause of all sorrow and suffering, both personally and collectively. The mind cannot be otherwise. It can only doubt. Doubting is its very nature.

Our organs of perception and action have a thousand and one limitations. Still, we question even God, the transcendental reality. Krishna, Rama and the Buddha were all great spiritual masters who were one with God, who embodied God's unconditional love, omniscience and divine beauty. People didn't spare them such criticism, either. Now, we have Amma with us. Even while watching the pada puja, while chanting archana, while meditating on her, or being in Amma's divine presence, our mind raises questions and doubts. Why? Because with our limited comprehension, we keep forgetting the infinite nature of Amma. The beautiful physical appearance of great masters is a veil that covers their real nature, which is sat-chit-ananda.

By nature, human beings look for immediate results. If someone advertises 'Enlightenment in ten days' or 'instant kundalini awakening,' we run after that. We don't mind spending hundreds, even thousands of dollars on such 'enlightenment' and 'awakening.' In doing so, we lose our common sense. We are so good in planning and managing everything in life, both enormous tasks as well as routine things such as our breakfast, lunch, dinner, outings, vacations, etc. But we act so unintelligently when it comes to spirituality and spiritual practices. We don't lend an ear to what the scriptures say, what the great sages and seers say…!

If enlightenment and unimpeded happiness were easily attainable, why did the great saints and sages—who gave us all the profound scriptures containing the ultimate experience of God-realization—go to the trouble of performing years of severe austerity? Was the Buddha a fool to renounce all the royal pleasures for attaining nirvana? Was Ramana Maharshi's grueling tapas inside the Pathala Lingam, an underground vault, meaningless? Was Sri Ramakrishna's intense longing and continuous prayers to Mother Kali a pointless drama?

What about Amma's years of intense meditation, prayers, chanting, and forgoing food and sleep as a little girl? Even Sri Krishna and Sri Rama meditated, observed vows and performed spiritual practices. In light of all this, what sort of 'instant enlightenment and kundalini awakening' are self-proclaimed gurus talking about?

Amma guarantees Self-realization in three years, maybe in even lesser time, provided we follow her instructions strictly, unfailingly, and with absolute trust. But effort is required. Ultimately though, we realize that even the effort wasn't necessary because we were never separate from God in the first place.

Amma's whole intention is to break the self-made wall we have created within us. The ego is very dear to us. We are so attached to it, whereas a Satguru such as Amma loves shattering egos. She is constantly trying to create at least a crack. If a crack appears, she knows that love and light will pour forth through that. Then the whole process of self-unfoldment becomes easy.

We have been living with our own ideas about life, love, the world, knowledge, etc. Meeting a Satguru such as Amma is the beginning of our entry into the path of purity and self-transformation. It is the beginning of our inward journey. For this journey to be successful, we must drop our incorrect ideas about life, love, the world, knowledge and all the information we have gathered. Amma lovingly tells her children, "My darling children, you don't need anything from outside.

Nothing has to be given, but many things have to be removed."

The law of worldly achievements and spiritual attainment are diametrically opposite. Your success in the world depends on acquisition, amassing wealth. The more you acquire, the more you succeed. In spirituality, conversely, losing is the law. You have to lose your ego and the negativities associated with it, the so-called veil that covers the truth of existence. One has to lose *ajnana* (ignorance) to gain jnana (true knowledge). In other words, *asat* (that which is not the real Self), has to be renounced to gain *sat* (the real Self or Atma).

Even to gain worldly things, one has to sacrifice many things that he or she considers dear.

Let me quote Amma, "In preparation for final exams, a student will only be able to focus on studies and get good grades if he relinquishes his habit of watching TV, going to movies, hanging out with friends, playing games and other entertainments. Sacrificing something of lesser significance to accomplish a higher goal is normal even in the world. What to say about the highest of all attainments, spiritual realization?"

So far, we have lived life valuing the numerous things we collected from the world, considering them to be precious. That was the true treasure for us. That perception needs to be corrected. We need an urgent surgery for this *ajnana timiram,* the cataract of ignorance. The surgery does involve some pain. But only if we allow Amma to flush out the unwanted things, will the hidden spiritual treasure within us reveal itself.

Gurus who claim to bestow enlightenment may let you keep all your ego embellishments, the misconceptions you have accumulated. Most people are happy about this, because that is what they want, albeit unconsciously. When you are keen to fulfill your desires and expectations, it is quite natural for you to end up with a 'master' who says, 'yes' to all your wishes. On the contrary, a real master may not pay any heed to your expectations, especially if your goal is Self-realization.

The most unfortunate thing is that those who are in search of freedom fall an easy victim to deceitful gurus. Their promises bind you ever more in the shackles of your wrong notions regarding spirituality and God-realization.

Remember this: You can choose any path, but without love, nothing works. Be it any yoga, bhakti, karma, or jnana — whatever it is — the common element is love. That is why Amma says, "Bhakti is love with jnana as its base." Otherwise, we will have the wrong perspective of Amma and spirituality. That, indeed, was the fundamental difference between the gopis and Radha. The gopis had love for Krishna, but they didn't have jnana about Krishna's all-pervasive nature, whereas Radha's love for Krishna was based on unshakeable faith in the Lord's all-knowing nature.

Our attitude shouldn't be, "Amma, I will stay with you only so long as you fulfill my wishes, expectations and make me feel happy. Otherwise, I will leave."

This attitude is not going to help us on the path. There is no bargaining in spirituality, especially with a Satguru such as Amma. In this path, only pure love and surrender will solve all the mysteries.

In 1983, I was physically away from Amma when she sent me to Tirupati, Andhra Pradesh, to take my master's degree exams in philosophy. The physical separation from Amma was so painful.

My heart was very heavy. In the train I sat in a corner to hide my tears. All the passengers were chatting cheerfully, but my mind was full of sorrow to be separated from Amma. Throughout the trip, I thought of nothing else but her.

Having reached there, I tried to concentrate on my studies but failed. I felt like a fish out of water. Every single object, a piece of paper, a matchbox, the yarn I used to tie around the packages I brought, the bag, the smell of every object reminded me of Amma. I forgot to eat and sleep. By the time the final exams began, I somehow managed to write the papers. At that time, I received a letter from Mother. Several times I read and reread it. Soaked by my tears, the letter turned wet. Mother's letter to me read:

> Darling Son,
> Amma is always with you. Amma doesn't feel that you are away from her. My child, Amma sees your yearning heart. She can hear your cries. My son, look at the trees dancing in the breeze, listen to the singing of the birds, gaze at the expanse of the sky, watch the twinkling stars, the mountains, valleys, rivers. They are all

manifestations of God. Everything in creation is filled with God's fragrance. See Amma in everything around you and be happy...

That night I was sitting outside my room, watching the trees and plants. The sky was full of glittering stars, and the silver light of the full moon flooded the entire earth. As tears streamed down my cheeks, my heart soared. I thought, 'This breeze may blow to my Amma; it may be fortunate enough to caress my Amma's body. The moon and the stars must also be longing to see Amma. Maybe they are also searching for her...' I could smell Amma in the breeze... There was a tangible presence of her everywhere. In that moment, I sang spontaneously:

> *tārā pathangaḷē tāzhōṭṭu pōrumō*
> *tārāṭṭu pāṭuvān ammayuṇḍu*
> *tīrātta snēhattin nīruravāṇavaḷ*
> *tēṭum manassinu taṇaḷānavaḷ*

O stars, can't you please come down?
Amma is here to sing a lullaby to you.
She is the stream of never-ending love and

She is the shade-giving tree for seeking
minds.

When I vacated the room after the exams, I
couldn't leave behind the useless newspapers,
which I had used as a wrapper to bring things
from the ashram, a broken piece of a soap box, the
empty bottles, the burnt-out tips of the incense
sticks, all the yarn I used to tie the packages, and
other 'throw-away' insignificant things. I thought,
"How intense was my pain when I was separated
from Amma! Perhaps these things, too, share that
pain; if I leave them here, they will be heartbroken." They didn't seem like lifeless objects to me.
So, I carefully packed those things in my bag as
well. Amma gave me a glimpse of what pure love
was, the state of gopi-hood, so to speak. If only
I could have maintained that state of mind, I
would have become her Radha—I mean, totally
one with her. I am sure, someday, it will happen.

There is a Sanskrit word, 'kataksha,' which
means, graceful glance. In Amma's *dhyana sloka*
(benedictory verse), she is described as '*snig-
dhāpāngavilokinīm bhagavatīm*' (whose glances
beam with binding love). The *Sri Lalita Sahas-*

*ranama* describes Devi as, *'Katakshakinkaribhoota kamalaakoti sevita'* (She who is attended by crores of Lakshmis, who are subdued by her simple glance).

You will find this word 'kataksha' in many of Amma's bhajans. The closest we can translate this word into English is 'glance' not 'look.' Even though we normally use 'glance' about certain ways of people looking at each other, in fact, 'glance' is something that God, the guru alone, can do because it comes from a totally different level.

There are moments when Amma glances at us. It is not a mere look. You will feel the difference. It is a secret communication between Amma and that particular person. No one else will be aware of it. The glance has to be earned. We have to be ready for it. When lovers fall in love, they experience a glimpse of that glance. It is not as intense or transformative as the guru's glance. But they get an idea about the difference between a look and a glance.

To put it in Amma's own words, "When the guru glances at the disciple, it is as though you are being enveloped by pure consciousness. The eternal abode of the guru is the highest plane of consciousness, the state of 'Shivoham' — 'I am Shiva.' From that peak, when the guru compassionately glances at the disciple, who is in a lower level of existence, the experience is like that of your whole being basking in an unbroken stream of torrential grace."

Occasionally, this happened to us when we first met Amma. The pure energy of that glance still remains within us. Once we are ready for total transformation, the guru's glance will push us into the totality of existence.

Amma says, "The true guru-disciple relationship is the peak of love and reverence."

When the disciple develops such love and reverence for his master, the very presence of the guru, even the guru's silence, communicates everything to the disciple. This is the meaning of Dakshinamurthy.[10]

_____

10 Dakshinamurthy' literally means 'one who faces the south.' A manifestation of Lord Shiva, Dakshinamurthy is regarded as the Adi Guru (or primordial guru). He is usually depicted as a young boy sitting under a banyan tree, and he imparts the highest wisdom to his disciples through silence.

For all this to happen, the disciple should have tremendous patience. "Have trust, be prepared and wait patiently," should be a disciple's mantra. "Speed thrills but kills" is a road sign we see in many places in India. This is a principle that is not only valid on the road, but in life also. Knowledge dawns within, but just as pregnancy and giving birth involve a great amount of patience, so too, the dawning of true knowledge demands immense patience.

When the disciple performs guru seva, he or she develops an identification with the guru. The guru's body is the base through which the disciple beholds God's love, purity, compassion, patience, forgiveness, self-sacrifice and all the divine qualities. The guru's body is, indeed, God's body, therefore, service to the guru is of paramount importance.

A fully surrendered disciple, even a disciple who has a degree of discernment, will not ask for anything from the guru. Such a disciple will not even say, "Bless me with enlightenment." Faith in the guru is the foundation of the guru-disciple relationship. The all-knowing guru knows what to impart to the disciple and when. For this reason, the disciple is supposed to trust the guru completely, do his sadhana, perform selfless service to the guru and wait lovingly and patiently for the guru's grace to flow.

The guru is infinite. His knowledge is also infinite. There is a famous verse in praise of the guru which goes like this, "If one has the guru's grace, one need not study every branch of knowledge, for all knowledge and its import will dawn within, of its own accord. To that guru's feet I humbly bow down."

Even though some of you have heard the following experience, I would like to share it with you. It was the occasion of Guru Purnima. A long time ago, back in early 80's, I had an intense desire to play the harmonium to accompany my own singing, for I felt that if I could play the harmonium while I sang, it would help me merge more deeply into the mood of love and devotion. I had been trying again and again and again. Every day, without fail I tried to play the instrument, but was not able to play anything more than the ascending and descending notes. One morning, while sitting inside the temple, I was going over my usual scales. Shortly after I began, Amma walked over to me and said, "I will teach you." She sat down next to me, and just like a teacher helping a child write the alphabet, Amma most affectionately held my fingers and pressed them down on the keys. Having done this only once, Mother got up and left, saying, "That is enough."

I thought this was just another playful moment created by Amma, another fond moment with Mother. I never dreamt that this one harmonium 'lesson,' which lasted only a few seconds, was going to make a miracle happen. The next day, there was an incident when I acted without discernment, for which Amma scolded me. Though I thought her displeasure ended with the scolding, I slowly realized that she was giving me 'the silent treatment.' It lasted for a couple of weeks, if I remember correctly. Needless to say, I was in deep sorrow, though the 'lesson' was much needed for me to realize my mistake.

The agony I felt inside inspired me to write a song. As I was writing down the lyrics, the melody came simultaneously to my mind. Shortly after, the song was written and set to music. At this point I had a strong urge to play it on the harmonium. It was as if someone had asked me to play it. I sat down and tried to play the harmonium. To my amazement, I found that I was spontaneously pressing the right keys. I couldn't believe that such skill could have developed in such a short time. But I knew it was Amma's grace that flowed through my fingers. It was Amma's divine touch that enabled me to play the instrument and thus fulfill my desire. That was the genesis of the song, *Nilambuja Nayane*.

> *nīlāmbuja nayanē ammē nī ariññō*
> *ī nīrunna cittattin tēngalukaḷ*
> *ētō janmattil cēytoru karmattāl*
> *ēkāntanāyi ñān alayunnu*

O Mother with the blue lotus eyes, will Thou not listen to the sobbing of this sorrowing heart. Perhaps, due to the deeds of some past birth, I am wandering alone.

Simply being in Amma's presence is tapas. We may not be aware, but it is purifying us, uplifting us, taking us closer to God, our true Self. Every moment we spend with Amma is like taking one step further towards the goal.

In fact, it is not correct to say "the disciple is seeking the guru." In reality, it is the other way around, "the guru is seeking the disciple." Why? Because the path of Self-realization and that ultimate experience is totally unknown to the disciple. Hence, the disciple does not have the wisdom to seek the guru, who is ever absorbed in that state of pure awareness. How can the ignorant seek pure knowledge? How can grief seek perfect bliss? So, the guru seeks the disciple. If the disciple is sincere in his approach, obedient to the guru, listens to the guru's teachings, practices them unfailingly by doing his sadhana as instructed by the guru, then no doubt, wonders will happen in the disciple's life, on his path to self-unfoldment.

In our total ignorance, we try to assess the way God operates with our limited mental and intellectual capabilities. Remaining within the premises of our diminutive world of understanding, we proudly feel that we can measure the immeasurable, whereas God with a snap of His finger wipes out all our ideas about life and the world. We see everything upside down.

Allow me to quote Lord Krishna from the *Bhagavad Gita*:

*ūrdhva-mūlam adhaḥ-śākham aśvattham*
*prāhur avyayam*

With roots above and branches below,
the banyan tree is said to be imperishable.
(15.1)

This upside-down tree is an allegory. From a tiny
seed manifests a gigantic banyan tree. It grows
and branches out almost like a miniature forest.
Some of the branches stoop so low as to touch
the ground. Out of them grow more roots. They
go deep into the soil from which a number of
supplementary branches stem out. Likewise, is
the human mind and numerous thoughts and
emotions. Every one of us is carrying a huge tree
of samsara within.

When we look into a pond or lake, we can see
the reflection of the trees growing on its banks.
What if we give reality to the reflection, forgetting
the real trees? This is our current state. We have
forgotten our true nature.

No matter who we are, rich or poor, educated
or uneducated, healthy or sick, we are all entan-
gled in this upside-down tree of samsara. We
never see our existence as it really is. We do not

see its beginning, middle or end. It is, in fact, a gigantic illusion that has been given reality due to the long-standing ignorance of our true nature.

We simply live out our lives in the endless chain of attraction to sense objects, desire, action, result and further desire. Amma compassionately offers to uplift us from this deluded state of mind.

There is a famous verse in the *Bhagavad Gita*. It is a tradition to chant this particular verse at the end of every chapter.

> *sarvadharmān parityajya mām ēkam*
> *śaraṇam vraja*
> *aham tvām sarva pāpēbhyō mōkṣayiṣyāmi*
> *mā śucaḥ*

> Abandon all varieties of dharmas and simply surrender unto me alone. I shall liberate you from all sins; do not fear. (18.66)

Just as this was Krishna's promise to the world, to his devotees, this is also Amma's promise to her children: "My darling children, Amma's love for you is endless. Amma cares for each one of you with no expectations, whatsoever. Learn to surrender. Amma will free you from the ocean of grief (*samsara sagaram*)."

Arjuna was confused about his dharma and thus thought the impending war was *adharma* (unjust). Standing at the warfront, he acted like a coward and wanted to flee. However, Krishna, the perfect master, instilled courage in him and awakened him to the reality of the situation. He imparted the highest spiritual knowledge to Arjuna and taught him how to view the whole event from a higher realm of consciousness. Krishna's most insightful guidance brought Arjuna back to his senses. He realized that the war wasn't his choice, but predetermined. This conviction helped Arjuna welcome the situation with self-surrender, thereby enabling him to use his full potential, without feeling any guilt or self-reproach.

May we be able to see Amma perfectly. May we be able to listen to Amma perfectly. May we be able to feel Amma perfectly. May we be able to love Amma perfectly, and may we be able to experience Amma perfectly.

Amma calls to us, "Darling children, come quickly. You are the essence of the eternal OM." Each one of us is 'darling' to God, to Amma and to the world. We each have so much to contribute. We just need to awaken and unleash the inner potential. So, remember that each one of us is important. Our life counts, and we can make a difference in this world.

Let us pray:

O Amma,
May your graceful glance help me to welcome all situations of life cheerfully.
May your graceful glance help me discharge my duties as a loving and selfless seva, rather than a chore.
May your graceful glance help me not to dwell in the past and the future, but to be in the present moment.
May your graceful glance help me to create the much-needed change within me, rather than focusing on changing others.
May your graceful glance help me to always remain content and happy in all circumstances of life.

*Aum Tat Sat* — That is the Truth.

CPSIA information can be obtained
at www.ICGtesting.com
Printed in the USA
FFHW010835251019
55717693-61615FF